THE
UNSPOKEN TRUTHS
for
CAREER SUCCESS

THE
UNSPOKEN TRUTHS
for
CAREER SUCCESS

Navigating Pay, Promotions,
and Power at Work

TESSA WHITE

HARPERCOLLINS
LEADERSHIP

AN IMPRINT OF HARPERCOLLINS

Published by HarperCollins Leadership, an imprint of HarperCollins Focus LLC.

Book design by Aubrey Khan, Neuwirth & Associates, Inc.
Magic Wand by Jo from Noun Project

Any internet addresses, phone numbers, or company or product information printed in this book are offered as a resource and are not intended in any way to be or to imply an endorsement by HarperCollins Leadership, nor does HarperCollins Leadership vouch for the existence, content, or services of these sites, phone numbers, companies, or products beyond the life of this book.

ISBN 978-1-4002-3601-5 (eBook)
ISBN 978-1-4002-3600-8 (PBK)

Library of Congress Cataloging-in-Publication Data
Library of Congress Cataloging-in-Publication application has been submitted.

Printed in the United States of America

HB 04.05.2023

To Kevin, my biggest fan from the beginning and the one who said this was not only possible, it was what I was intended to do. To my children: Zac, Jantzen, Hannah, Whitney, Kayla, and Gentry. They never gave me a hard time when I locked myself in my office for weeks and put Mom duty on the back burner for a season. Lastly, to Stephie. She likes to remind me she's the only friend left who could put up with my ridiculous work schedule. Our morning run to McDonald's before the writing day started was the only time we could play together, and her sacrifice must be noted.

CONTENTS

Preface ix

1. Something's Got to Give 1

2. The Problem with Companies 19

3. The Problem with People 39

4. Lies About Performance 57

5. Lies About Power 83

6. Lies About the Corner Office 103

7. Getting Comfortable with Conflict 121

8. Lies About Promotability 143

9. Promotability: Early-Stage Careers 155

10. Promotability: Mid-Stage Careers 167

11. Promotability: Senior Leadership 179

12. Lies About Pay 195

13. Lies About Leverage 209

14. Lies About Company Loyalty 229

15. Lies About Burnout 253

16. Lies About Politics 267

Conclusion: Should I Stay or Should I Go? 285

Endnotes 305

Index 309

About the Author 319

PREFACE

My daughter was the one who convinced me to post on TikTok. She was sure that my career advice was something that would resonate with the millennial generation. As skeptical as I was, I gave her the green light to post a few videos. Then I all but forgot about it. Three days later my son called from California and said, "Mom, my girlfriend just called and swears she saw you on Tik-Tok. Is that even possible?" I logged in and found that I had ten thousand followers. Two years later, I have over a million followers on my social channels, and I receive more than two hundred messages a day from individuals scattered across the career spectrum. It has blown my mind.

Moving from the corporate side of business to helping individuals navigate their workplace has been one of the most natural transitions of my career. In fact, my husband tells everyone that on our first blind date together, he asked me career advice and immediately dubbed me the "Ask Tessa" hotline. It must have been good advice because he hasn't let me out of his sight since that night. He has been my most ardent supporter.

I was lucky enough to start my career with Stephen R. Covey at the age of twenty-two. He changed my life in more ways than one. His teachings on life and leadership shaped me and helped me navigate my own murky career waters as a single mother of three young children. If you hear undertones of his work in my book, you'll know why. I considered him a mentor and his principles a lifesaver to me.

My last corporate role was at Vivint Solar (now Sunrun), a company made up of about four thousand young millennials. There were only about a dozen of us that were over forty. I loved my time there and it helped me tap into the needs of a younger generation and see firsthand how they absorbed information.

From Vivint Solar, my teaching style evolved and is made up of quick, actionable nuggets. I realized that people didn't need someone sharing grandiose frameworks and philosophies. They were clamoring for "learning snacks" rather than a full meal, quick answers and scripts to use in common workplace situations. My book reads more like a CliffsNotes version of a career bible.

I cannot promise that after you read this book you'll shift from career burnout to job nirvana. After all, if we are growing, our jobs will inherently challenge us. But if you utilize the tools, scripts, and techniques I've outlined, it will make a meaningful difference to how others at work (and especially your managers) perceive you. In turn, the relationship you have with the workplace will change for the better. You will reclaim some workplace satisfaction and begin stacking victories in your own career corner.

I owe a debt of gratitude to those who lifted me through this process: first and foremost, my husband, Kevin, and our six grown children, who let me lock myself in my office for a year to write this. I also owe Wendy Keller and Jenn Dorsey the equivalent of a firstborn child, for the heavy lift they both gave to the project. Without them, there would be no book. And lastly, my dear friends and colleagues—Bryan Christiansen, Jeremy Sabin, Steve Littlefield, and Loki Mulholland—all geniuses in their own right and contributors to the content and ideas.

THE
UNSPOKEN TRUTHS
for
CAREER SUCCESS

1

Something's Got to Give

've been promoted. I've been affected by a reorganization and I've been fired. I've gotten the job. I've not gotten the job. I've negotiated a great pay package and I have undernegotiated and learned that all of my coworkers were paid more than I was. At different times I have been labeled a top performer and an average performer. I've been called a micromanager. I've also been called "the best leader I ever had in my career."

I've taken risks that have paid off and gotten me promoted, and I've had epic failures. I've had some of the most wonderful mentors and managers I could have wished for—including working with Stephen R. Covey in my first career role. And I've had managers that made workdays feel as if I were walking through mud for ten hours straight.

You and I really aren't that different from each other. You have a similar list of ups and downs already building in your career, and many of the difficulties you'll encounter will chip away at your overall job satisfaction. They may even cause you to seek a new opportunity, a better job, a better boss, or a better work environment. But no matter where you land, your list of workplace frustrations will be there.

I know I'm not the only one who has felt that something has to give.

My own tipping point took my breath away. We knew our daughter was not doing well and that suicide was a possibility. It weighed heavily on us. It wasn't *the* reason I took a hard look at my work life, but it certainly was a factor. I was balancing the needs of several grown children in distress while working as a senior executive at a fast-paced company that we had just taken public and was still growing at an astounding rate. To say that I was overwhelmed and burned out is an understatement.

The decision I made to temporarily walk away from my job was deliberate but still one of the hardest ones of my career. I remember walking into the CEO's office at the end of the day, having scheduled time to talk when others would not be around.

"I need to take a leave of absence. Starting tomorrow."

I still remember the taste of those words coming out. It was as if they were on a string that I immediately wanted to pull back into my mouth. I was terrified of what this would mean for my place in the company and for my career. But the choice was made. I said it out loud, making it a reality.

One day later, our daughter attempted suicide.

I returned to work ten weeks later, grateful our daughter was still with us. But I was changed forever. This time, work was more deliberate, more on my terms. I had a difficult time reengaging and reclaiming some satisfaction from work. I was SVP of Human Capital—a great role that had taken me twenty-plus years to grow into. But now, struggling with the aftereffects of an unpredictable turn, life and work felt like too much.

The leave of absence and my return to work shaped my decision to begin to uncouple myself from my career over the next year and a half. My plan was to leave the corporate side of human resources and help others navigate the challenges of the workplace and reclaim some control over their career growth.

I don't think my internal struggle with where I fit in the workplace was unique. I'm not the only one whose personal and work lives had become enmeshed. I'm not the only one who sought answers for how to reclaim some sanity. We live in a complicated world, and it affects all of us.

In my own circle, I don't have to look far to see people struggling to fit into the workplace. I have a neighbor who is a highly educated healthcare provider, but he's working at an Amazon warehouse right now because he is so burned out. My husband has switched from a home office to a work office and back again half a dozen times. He used to travel more than 50 percent of the time, but as of this writing he hasn't been on an airplane in two years. My sister runs her own small business. She went from two stores to one and can barely keep it open because finding good entry-level help at a reasonable wage is impossible.

According to the American Psychological Association, nearly three in five employees reported negative impacts of work-related stress, with 36 percent reporting cognitive weariness, 32 percent reporting emotional exhaustion, and an astounding 44 percent reporting physical fatigue—a 38 percent increase since 2019.[1]

Then there is me. I'm now a "reformed" executive, who, at the height of my career, left the corner office to spend my days teaching people how to understand and navigate their companies.

Feeling good about our workplaces has never been easy. The rat race is getting rattier. It's going in the wrong direction, and fast.

Surveys say that anywhere from 51 percent to over 65 percent of people are disengaged from the workforce. With these odds, I'm guessing you relate.

BURNOUT: A GROWING PROBLEM

Earlier in my career, burnout wasn't even a "thing." We didn't have language to describe it until the publication of the Maslach Burnout Inventory (MBI) in 1981. But the MBI has become a useful tool for companies to assess employee burnout and categorize it as a true organizational issue in line with the World Health Organization's definition of burnout. The MBI definition focuses on three elements:

1. Feelings of low energy or exhaustion
2. Increased cynicism or negativity about one's job
3. Reduced efficacy at work

Burnout isn't a new problem, but it's a growing problem. Long before it had specific criteria to define it, I had felt it and watched others grapple with it in the workplace. Christina Maslach, a professor emerita of psychology at the University of California, Berkeley, and the world's foremost expert on burnout, describes it this way: "It's rarely something that affects an individual alone; it's not just about workload. It's about how much control you have, and it's also affected by the extent to which you get recognized and rewarded for doing good things as opposed to 'a good day is a day when nothing bad happens.'"

I relate to this, and I know that many others feel the pressures of the workplace weighing them down and want to retain their sense of control.

Right now there is a "global picket line" between employers and employees: it has many names, including the Great Resignation, the Big Quit, the Great Reshuffle, and the Great Questioning.[2] Whatever name ends up sticking isn't the important part. What is important is finding out what is causing a majority of individuals to rethink work.

If you are among those who aren't satisfied but can't quite crack the code on how to reclaim workplace satisfaction, you're not alone. Everywhere I look, people are searching for answers. They want to take back control of their careers, not just sit back and let their careers happen. Given that your time at work often equals or surpasses your time at home, being dissatisfied for more than half your waking hours isn't an acceptable way to live. The workplace will continue to shift and change. Regaining some control so you can at least help steer your career—even if you aren't fully in the driver's seat—may be a way to reclaim some sanity at work.

I have a few secrets to share about regaining some control. Many people are not aware of the invisible rules of the road that govern the workplace. It's my goal to share with you what they are to help you create more frictionless career growth. I want you to have greater clarity on how the workplace works because all too often individuals don't accurately interpret what they see or experience. Once the curtain is drawn back and you can see the dynamics that are in play, it's like suddenly finding the missing instruction manual to a piece of IKEA furniture. You still have to do the work, but doing it with the manual at least gives you a fighting chance.

I am offering up a powerful reframe about the lies you've believed so far in your career and helping you replace them with the truths that really govern the workplace. Imagine a workplace manual for how to unpack the most common conflicts and frustrations individuals experience in the workplace—from work-life balance, to pay inequities, to difficult work politics, to how to handle conflict without putting your job at risk. It may feel like an impossible wish list, but there are strategies and tools that can put you back in the driver's seat of your career.

WHY SHOULD YOU BELIEVE THE JOB DOCTOR?

Starting as a young secretary and a single mother of three, I scraped my way to a senior executive role in a Fortune 50 company by starting as an administrative assistant with no college degree. It sounds so easy when I see it in a nice concise sentence like that—as if I just started working and in a blink, I made it to the top. The real journey was incredibly difficult with chapters of sadness, victory, and frustration, probably not unlike your own experience.

But this isn't just about my own journey. I'm offering insight into the tens of thousands of careers I've overseen in my role as the head of human resources. I have something unique to offer to those making their own way in the workplace. My brain contains a massive database of hirings and firings, pay information and negotiation techniques, and an insider's view of the interactions between a company and its people, which has helped me identify patterns in the workforce.

I have a front-row seat to careers like yours, all the behind-the-scenes conversations, and the deals made behind closed doors. This information has changed how I see the workforce. If you don't believe my journey, I hope you'll believe the journey of the many others who have come before you.

If careers were easy, I wouldn't be in business as the Job Doctor. Honestly, I wish it were easier for everyone to navigate their careers: to get the jobs they want, get raises when they help their companies succeed, and be energized by making a difference in the places where they choose to apply their talents and time. But unfortunately, careers and companies are complicated. People get stuck. What "stuck" looks like is as varied as the people in the workplace. Sometimes it takes the form of not getting the promotion you feel you deserved. Other times it's feeling as if you've been taken advantage of—that you're working harder without getting commensurate rewards for the effort.

Reclaiming your workplace satisfaction isn't always accomplished by hopping from one job to another. You also don't have to just grin and bear it when you are miserable.

You may be wondering where that leaves you. My answer is that you are on the edge of a big epiphany about your choices. It starts with realizing what you thought you knew about the workforce isn't true.

You are misguided.

That's a bold statement—until you consider the fact that I've seen your workplace grievance thousands of times. I've seen it from multiple points of view: yours, your manager's, and the company's. I can see where human behavior converges with common workplace issues and how situations will play out either in favor (or, more often, *not* in favor) of you, the person who comes to work each day trying to earn a living and make a difference.

If you are thinking "The workplace is permanently broken and nothing I can do will change that," I hear you loud and clear. You can't "fix" it. If that were possible, it would have been done already. But you can move within it more effortlessly when you understand workplace principles better. Let me show you the magic of reframing how you think it works against you and how it actually can work *for* you. Let me help you dispel the lies and uncover the truths.

Unless you know the right levers to push and pull,
the workplace will empty you as much as it fills you.

Nothing you or I do will *cure* the workplace. But when I reveal how decisions are made and introduce the guardrails that can help you steer away from career trouble, your workplace satisfaction will take big leaps forward and fewer steps back. It will help you make better decisions. You will avoid the potholes that can stall out your career progression. You will navigate your current job more effectively, but it may also nudge you toward deciding to leave your company in search of something better. Either way, I am offering a lens by which to see and understand the workplace better. I can give you the truth. And the truth can indeed set you free:

- Free to make more informed career decisions
- Free to have better discussions with your manager
- Free to move through conflict without putting your job at risk
- Free to get the pay you deserve
- Free to see what's coming next in your career and how to prepare for it

You get to decide if you want to implement (or even believe) what I'm telling you about creating a better work experience and fulfilling career. Not everybody will implement every tool or resource in this book. You may also find that you need to make some modifications so that the approaches—especially the scripts

I share—feel authentic to you. Consider the tools and ideas a starting point for your individualized journey.

WHERE ARE YOU IN YOUR CAREER?

If you are new in your career: I suspect you are trying to get your footing solid underneath you and set yourself up for some good career growth. I imagine you have enough exposure to the workplace to wonder how you will survive this crazy train and whether you've picked the right career or industry. You may be considering whether you can make it as a contractor or gig worker doing what you love, starting your own business, or how long you need to stay in your current role before you move on.

If you are in the middle stage of your career: You've had some success and now you find yourself in the hardest part of your career— stuck in the middle. You may find yourself trapped between the senior team and their demands (which seem rooted in something other than reality) and the career newbies who think they should have your job. You may be looking at whether you really want to follow a manager track or if a path exists for an individual contributor that doesn't penalize you financially.

If you are a new senior leader: You are likely in a pressure cooker, fighting for relevancy day and night. You may be wondering if there is a tipping point after which it gets easier. You've had some successes to get to this level, but I'm guessing you don't feel that you have it all figured out yet despite the title you hold. You may be wondering whether a few more years will put you on a glide path to the future or if it will be more of the same.

The workplace doesn't just fall into place and work the way you think it should. There are no guarantees that time in a role will move you up in an organization. Nor are there guarantees the company you've selected will be any better than your last workplace. The only thing I can tell you for sure is that the journey will be messier than you hope. And to navigate the rough terrain, you need to know the difference between a lie and the truth.

THE LIES AND TRUTHS OF THE WORKFORCE

I'm a believer in looking the facts straight in the face.

It seems natural that if we were all looking at the same thing, we would be able to see it in a similar way. But all it takes is watching the news on two different channels to realize that the facts may be the same, but the conclusions we draw are vastly different. The same is true in the workforce. We assign meaning to what happens at work, which may or may not be the same meaning that another person assigns.

My years in human resources have helped me see different sides of the same coin and understand the varied perspectives that individuals can bring to the same experience. Here's an example of what that might look like:

Manager: *I'm getting frustrated with Evan's work. He used to be such a problem-solver, but lately I feel like he's waiting for me to tell him what to do, and he has lost his drive. I need team members who understand what accountability looks like and aren't waiting on someone else to tell them what to do.*

Evan: *I was hired for my expertise in this area, but I quickly learned my manager wasn't interested in ideas. He wants someone to do it his way, even if better alternatives exist. He is the ultimate micromanager. I get so tired of redoing work. I wish he would trust me to just take it and run.*

The fact is that Evan is disengaging, but the reasons why are completely different to each person. This is only one illustration of that disconnect, but I could write hundreds of examples that show how quickly we get on different pages at work and how we interpret— often incorrectly—what is actually happening.

So let's rip the covers off the lies and dysfunctions of the workplace and replace your false beliefs with a more truthful version. It is a mighty game changer.

Some of the lies of the workforce will give you new insight. Some will make you angry.

For example, on my TikTok account I commented on a recruiter's Instagram post regarding pay negotiation. My post alone had more than seven million views in four days. Her post was picked up by all the major news outlets, and in true "cancel culture" form, her company was bombarded with calls for her immediate termination. She said this:

"I just offered a candidate $85,000 for a job that had a budget of $130,000. I offered her that because that's what she asked for. And I personally don't have the bandwidth to give lessons on salary negotiation. Here's the lesson. ALWAYS ASK FOR THE SALARY YOU WANT (DESERVE), no matter how large you think it might be. You never know how much money a company has to work with. #beconfident"

The responses from people were brutal! How dare a company pay someone so far under what the company was willing to pay! Companies are capitalist pigs!

You might not like to hear how companies make decisions. You may find it equally distasteful how compensation negotiations work. I would rather have you understand it than be disadvantaged throughout your career.

Other lies of the corporate world might not spark anger but may give you a great sense of relief once you know them. For example, having the tools to see company politics through a different lens gives you a whole framework with which to navigate your workplace successfully. Instead of vilifying corporate politics, you can see it for what it is: rules of the road that you can navigate to your advantage.

Regardless of how you feel and whether you like the lies and truths in your workplace, the benefits of knowing them are incredible. It has the potential to give you a better relationship with your manager, minimize burnout, and move from being seen as a steady performer to being seen as a difference maker. It will help you see the workplace through fresh eyes.

Instead of hoping you can find a company that provides the right setting, the right culture, or the right rules and processes, you can understand how to look at the workplace altogether differently, with the data points from thousands of careers as your guide. To do that, we'll explore some of the most common lies and truths you might tell yourself at work:

Lies about performance. You don't know the truth about how others perceive you. Every single piece of feedback you hear is a watered-down version of how you are really perceived. Learn to stop waiting on the company and create the conditions for honest feedback.

Lies about promotability. It's easy to be lulled into thinking you are adding value when you are just getting work done. Learn to rely less on a job description and instead understand how to practice the right skill set for the next stage of career growth that can earn you a seat at the table.

Lies about your pay. Many of us believe that if we work hard enough, we will be rewarded with greater pay, but the truth is that just doing your job will keep you safe but will never be enough to get you meaningful advances in pay. Stop focusing on ineffective pay increase strategies like year-end reviews and instead learn what leverage is and how to use it to maximize your pay.

Lies about power. Company power doesn't solely lie in titles, corner offices, or the size of the staff. The language of business is numbers, and those who can translate their asks and their results by using data and specialized knowledge are the ones who gain entry into decision-making circles.

Lies about loyalty. We think companies will return the loyalty we give, but that isn't how they are designed. They will take as much as you are willing to give. Once you realize that finding balance is your job and not the company's, you can adopt a far more balanced practice and never again be more loyal to a company than it can be to you in return.

Lies about burnout. We often look at burnout in a one-dimensional way and believe if we could only do less work, the problem would be fixed. That's only part of the truth. When we work *with* our brains rather than *against* them, it opens up greater capacity and gives us one more control to minimize burnout.

Lies about politics. It's easy to think of politics as the enemy when they're actually an instruction manual for company success. Learn how to use company politics as a road map to the company values and how to get work across the finish line.

These lies and the truths that will replace them can help you have better conversations with your leaders, get more of your asks across the finish line, and read with greater clarity what is happening in your career. My dad would call it "greasing the skids." It's the skills combined with the guiding principles that will help you regain control.

WARNING INDICATOR LIGHTS IN YOUR CAREER

Much like personal or relationship problems, work problems can seem small until you don't address them, and then they get very big very fast. The same is true with careers. People ask me all the time how to know when something is wrong and changes need to be made.

Your biggest career warning is when
you see nothing happening.

If your line of sight to what's next in your career is a black hole, that's a good indication there is a problem, because the first place you need to look is at yourself and how clear you are on what you want. Sure, you might get lucky and stumble into a decent job, but that is not career strategy.

While there is no 100 percent accurate fail-safe list to gauge if you are off-track in your career, the one that follows has merit. With these warning indicators, sometimes there is an explanation, and sometimes it can mean nothing. If just one of these indicators is flashing, don't panic. Instead, watch for a pattern of multiple warning signs to tell you if there is something wrong in your career. If you relate to one item on the list, it may be a fluke. Seeing yourself in two of them may be a coincidence. But three is a pattern, and you better pay close attention.

CAREER WATCH-OUTS

- Neither your responsibilities nor your title have advanced for at least three years.
- Your "asks" are getting turned down.
- You have a lack of momentum and aren't hitting goals or objectives.
- Your pay has moved less than 10 percent over a five-year period.
- You don't have at least three senior-level advocates (people who would champion you).
- Your performance appraisals have multiple below-average ratings each year.

When the warning indicators go off, don't ignore them. They are lagging indicators, which means they have been brewing for a while. You are already late in realizing that you need to make some changes.

WHAT HAPPENED?

If you have several warning indicators in your career, you may be any of the following:

- A poor advocate for yourself, or you are waiting on the company to advocate for you
- Working hard but not strategically picking work the company will value
- Uncomfortable communicating through conflict
- Under the impression that creating boundaries for yourself or work-life balance is someone else's job
- Unclear on your ability to create influence or power in your role
- Blaming company politics instead of utilizing them correctly
- Unaware of how others experience you at work

Don't panic if you see yourself in this list. It's not too late to address the cause and create your own great turnaround plan. As is the case with growth and development, you are never done learning. You see it in professional sports where the best athletes in the world continue to get coached daily. They are constantly refining themselves. They don't learn something and then check it off their list and call it "done," nor should you.

So let's bust those doors open, address the lies you've been believing all this time, and uncover the truth of what is happening with your career. Open yourself up to the possibility that what drives you crazy in the workforce and is holding you back might not be what you think.

2

The Problem
with Companies

Lie: A company is the enemy to the individual.

Truth: A company isn't good or bad.
It is simply aligned with getting results.

got called when someone brought a tiger into the building. That's right: a tiger. To be fair, it was in a cage, but still—it was a tiger. Being in human resources has given me a front-row seat to thousands of stranger-than-life stories: An awkward conversation with an individual who was passing gas all day in their cubicle (surprisingly common). An employee who turned a company warehouse into a front for another business from which they ran a whole separate work team. Swinger and drug rings run out of the office, a surprise pregnancy (twins!) from an illicit affair between two married executives, and an unfortunate brush with poop art in the restroom (we called him the "Texas Crapper").

I could write a full book with story after story of the bizarre. In human resources, truth is indeed stranger than fiction.

The stories from my career may be unpredictable, but the way that companies behave and the choices they make are incredibly predictable. I suppose that is why, in part, I can be so effective in helping people with scripts and scenarios they can use in common situations. A client recently said to me, "If I didn't know better, I'd say you were a time traveler. You knew every single rebuttal my manager would have and how to respond. It's like you saw it in the future and brought the answers to me before it happened!" I'm not a magician and I have no secret time-travel skills. But with tens of thousands of employee issues under my belt, I know there is clearly a theme in how the company (and those representing it) will respond to any given situation.

The idea that you can predict how the company will behave and operate in most situations seems farfetched. I can't count how many times I've wished I had a manual for success in my career or relationships or parenting.

While I can't help with parenting or relationships, I can tell you that knowing the rules to which a company is aligned is as close as you get to a manual. I've heard people say that defining how to behave in a corporate environment is a "game" or "manipulative" or another similarly negative term. I disagree. Knowing how the company operates (and what it values) is no different from learning the rules of addition. Companies' decision-making processes are also as predictable as $2 + 2 = 4$. It's the people part that carries the variation. (Cue the tiger.)

A company's DNA doesn't change. Companies are what they are, and when you begin to understand them better, you can work within them in a less adversarial way. Rather than getting fed up and divorcing your company, do a little counseling here with me first. There may be a path where both you and your employer get what you want out of the relationship. When you are clear on what the company cares about, you'll know how to better predict their behavior. If you know your audience, you'll know your approach.

But first, a disclaimer.

Remember when I told you that some of the lies and truths of the workplace would make you angry? This is *that* chapter. A few more paragraphs in, and you are going to want to throw this book against the wall. But stick with me. There is tremendous power in understanding companies, even if it causes you to feel unsettled. As I peel back some basic truths, it isn't going to make you feel any better, at least until I get to the part about how you "get even." Let me rephrase that. You may want to get even, but evening out the relationship between employer and employee is what I mean to do. I don't want you to be on opposite sides of a dogfight with your employer—mostly because you'll lose. I want you to know how to work *with* a company to get what you need, rather than experiencing the friction that pits you *against* each other.

I would say that I'm on your side, except there isn't a side. Getting angry because a company is being a company is like getting annoyed when your dog barks at strangers. It's what dogs do. You can't expect your dog to act like a cat. Companies have characteristics that define them too. They aren't good or bad necessarily; they just "are." These characteristics are present in every decision that a company makes. Their top priority is to make a profit. They will always try to save money, fund what brings more sales, and push back against new expenses that eat away at profitability.

I love predictability, and companies are incredibly predictable! If you know what they are and what they are not, you can use that knowledge to your advantage rather than to your peril. For instance, if you decide to ask for a raise solely based on not having had a raise for several years, you will get a "no." Why? The company is not aligned to spend more money if it doesn't tie back to results. But if you asked for that same raise differently—making a clear connection between your contributions and company priorities—you just exponentially increased your odds for a "yes." Knowing the triggers for the company helps you better predict its behavior and how to position your own interactions. In other words, if you want to get what you are asking for, learn to speak their language.

The Scales Aren't Tipped in Your Favor

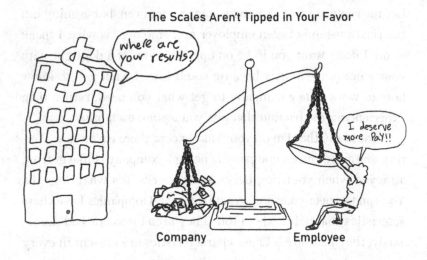

Cullyn Cowell

That doesn't mean you get nothing out of the arrangement and the company always comes out on top. On the contrary! Adjust your focus to what the company cares about—such as, "How do I get the company results?"—and it will likely point you toward solving or prioritizing a different set of problems than if you went to work thinking simply, "What's in my job description?" Even this one change will set you on a better path toward workplace satisfaction.

> *Alignments drive behavior.*
> *Understand alignments and you can predict behavior.*

Once you understand a company and the key relationships within it, such as managers and human resources, you'll have the basic skills required to collaborate with a company, not fight against it. In this chapter, I'll introduce you to the key stakeholders and give you the tools you need to understand them better.

WHAT'S IN IT FOR ME?

Aligning to a company's point of view provides a list of benefits that help erase barriers and create opportunities in the workplace.

- It will drive you to measure your own results more.
- It will change the way you ask for raises or propose ideas.
- It will shift the tasks you choose to prioritize.
- It will help you select the work that gives you the greatest leverage.
- It will adjust your language to that of a partner rather than an adversary.

AN EMPLOYEE, AN HR PERSON, AND A MANAGER WALKED INTO A BAR . . .

While it sounds like a start to a bad joke, this triumvirate stirs up all kinds of skepticism.

Yet these are the three groups that have to get along in any company. You'll have to pass through the manager and human resources before you can work any career magic. If you aren't clear on what they are aligned to do, it's a bit like being blindfolded and trying to make your way through a maze of folding chairs. Most people are striving for a workplace that feels supportive, yet these entities often seem to be working against the employee rather than moving in alignment with them. At times it feels as if you're in a game of dodgeball and the other team is ganging up on you. Throw in some dysfunctional company politics, shifting priorities, pressure from the top for results, manager shortcomings, and employee burnout, and you have a frustrating combination that can curl the toes of even the heartiest individuals. As dire as it may feel to the person stuck in the middle, it's not a lost cause.

If you want something, don't come at it from why you want it. Come at it from why the company benefits from it.

THE PROBLEM WITH COMPANIES

Companies are created for one reason: to make a profit. Let me quickly get past the disclaimer: Yes, even nonprofits must take in enough money to balance the books. Yes, some companies don't make a profit for a while, but it's only because they believe that if they go fast enough, there will be a lot of money in their future.

In other words, not having money is a short-term condition. The simple truth is that, over the long haul, no company can exist if it cannot eventually make money. I'm not saying it's right or even humane. But for today, it is what it is. This is the first and highest truth.

TRUTH (#1)
The company exists to make money.

If being profitable is the true nature of a company, then to reach that goal, its leaders will only make decisions that bring in more revenue, increase efficiency, or decrease costs. Yes, they can have a great mission to change the world, but no company gets to change the world if it is out of business. No money, no business.

TRUTH (#2)
The company only spends money if it helps with their bottom line.

If you forget that results are oxygen to a company and you believe that a company will make decisions that are good for you—and not for the company—you will be disappointed time after time. The sales department has favored status because revenue is the lifeblood of the company. Every single decision a company makes passes through the lens of *Does this expenditure help us make more or save more than we are spending?*

The tug-of-war begins when individuals want to be paid more. Or hire more people. Or invest in new tools and resources. This is great when you can show that it helps the company with Truth #1 or #2. But more times than not, people are thinking about it in intangible terms, such as, "If I'm happier at work, I'll produce more." Sounds great in principle, but a company will find it diffi-cult to invest in people or resources based on a loose promise of "producing more." Companies need a guaranteed return (or close to it) on their investments.

People love to hate their companies because it often feels like the company is trying to suck the life out of each person, but if you think about it, both you and the company will take as much as the other is willing to give. That's what you have in common. Both you and the company are trying to make a "profit" (for you, this means the return you make for the effort you put in). The company makes more profit by *not* paying you more. The company *not* paying you more hurts *your* ability to make a profit.

> *You aren't that different from the entity you*
> *love to hate. Neither you nor the company want*
> *to give unless you get something in return.*

You and the company are misaligned out of the gate. I can't change that, but I can help you understand the thought process of your employer so you can better position your own asks in a way that makes sense for the company. When you take a "what's in it for them" approach to your asks, you are likely to get a lot more of what you want as well. Here is a summary of what to expect from your employer.

WHAT YOU CAN EXPECT FROM YOUR COMPANY

More revenue is at the top of the priority list. That's why companies prioritize sales departments, technology (which creates efficiencies), and product development teams (which create new products that bring in revenue), and the support departments like finance, HR, and marketing have a harder time getting money from the company. They are a cost drain without bringing in revenue.

They always want something in return for their investment. That's why it's essential that you clearly identify the return on any investment (ROI) you are asking the company to make. The murkier the ROI, the less likely you'll get the money. It's the primary lens they use to make an investment decision.

They will push for doing more with less. They will always want the most for the least amount of money. More effort, less cost, every single time. This is why they'll take the option to see results first and then invest instead of the other way around.

They won't break with the approved budget lightly. They will rejigger the existing budget—steal from one department to fund another to adjust and reprioritize. But big changes to the budget are a big deal and must go to the board of directors. This is risky for a CEO to do, and they must be pretty bullish on the idea to take that risk.

How to Apply This Knowledge

This information helps you because when you know you have to frame your asks from the perspective of results first (backed by numbers), not good ideas (backed by feelings), then your requests become more aligned with how the company sees the world. Your feelings, such as "I'm burned out," don't mean a lot, because they're coming from *your* needs, not the company's. Think about how you can align your conversation to the company's needs.

Any time you want to get a "yes" from the company, you need to lead with the results and positive outcomes the *company* could get and not what *you* can get. Check out this example:

→ **The approach that would not work:** "I'm more productive from home." This does not address the proposal with hard facts or results that have any convincing depth.

→ **The approach that has a higher likelihood of success:** "My projects have all come in at least two weeks ahead of deadline since I've worked from home. I've also measured that I gain back 20 percent or eight additional hours of time each week that used to be taken up by office distractions. This time savings would allow me to get to the net promoter project we have not been able to fit into our schedule. If you will allow me to continue working from home, I believe I can prove out the productivity lift. To make sure it works for the company, let's check in after three months and see if this could be an ongoing arrangement that meets the company's needs."

→ **Why it works:** The company is unlikely to base a decision off your feeling that you are more productive. There is no specific data and the ask is based only on the individual's self-assessment. However, when the approach shifts to a specific savings per week, and the individual backs up their assertion with a clear way to show the efficiency uplift, it becomes more interesting to the company. The pot gets even sweeter when the individual positions it as an experiment with a measurement period, rather than a permanent change. Companies love experiments with an "out" if it doesn't work.

THE PROBLEM WITH MANAGERS

It's easy to blame managers for the bad experiences you have in the workplace because, as agents of the company, they are the ones you interact with most often. All the frustration one feels about the workplace is easy to put on the heads of those who carry the company torch. The statistics bear it out: the Society for Human Resources Management recently produced a survey that shows 84 percent of people blame poorly trained managers for their work stress, and more than 50 percent feel their own performance would improve if their manager knew more about how to manage people.

However, managers have a Job #1 (managing the budgets and team) that ties back to the company's Job #1 (getting results), and it isn't being your life coach or your work counselor.

TRUTH #3
Managers are aligned to hit their goals with the budget they have (which is never as much as they ask for).

If it doesn't sound very sexy, that's because it isn't.

Managers are the primary gatekeepers of the budgets; they are the project-completion watchdogs. Good managers do know that treating their people well will get them results. But this does not come without challenges, usually in the form of limited budgets and autonomy to make desired changes.

They do have limits to their autonomy, which many individuals don't realize. The title of manager does not give the full flexibility to make any decision they want with whatever resources they need. They have flexibility to access their own budget, but getting money outside of that requires them to get fairly uncomfortable fairly fast. Given that most managers (especially those at the director level or below) are handed a budget that was pared down from their original request (rather than getting the budget they believe they need), most special asks that require money create constraints right out of the gate.

They are also the point persons for people problems. This is no small task. Most data suggests this takes up about 20 percent of their time. These issues vary and it's tougher than it looks: time-off management, interpersonal conflict, performance issues, adjustments to projects, priorities, workflow, coworker disagreements—the list could go on and on. The problems that a manager faces don't always come with a manual of prescribed solutions. Managers have to make decisions every day that hopefully take care of the individual (without upsetting others on the team) and that also fit nicely into what human resources is aligned to do, which is to not create greater risk to the company, while still meeting budgets and goals. This complicated dance is often why managers will look to precedents—the way things have been done in the past—to make their decisions, and why many managers are hesitant to take a new or risky idea up the chain.

People in the workforce complain that their managers are out of touch, or too in touch (micromanagement). Managers are the number-one reason cited by employees for their poor work experience. According to the Predictive Index's 2021 People Management Report, 63 percent of employees surveyed who reported having a bad manager said they planned to leave their companies within the next year.

Yet, somehow, companies expect that if someone is a good individual contributor, they will make a good manager. I find it curious that despite the need for good managers and the abundance of bad manager complaints, building better managers seems to be an afterthought.

If you have a poorly trained manager, it will be incumbent on you to be even more intentional and clear in the proposals and asks you put forward. You will need to use rationale that is even *more* tightly aligned to the manager's Job #1 and clearly articulate how it helps the department or broader company. The best way to do this is to amplify the use of data in your argument and ensure it aligns to your manager's worldview as well as to that of the company and human resources. You are stacking the odds in your favor one more notch every time you provide rationale that speaks to the concerns of each entity.

WHAT YOU CAN EXPECT FROM MANAGERS

Motivated to stay within the budget. Managers really have to believe there is a substantive benefit for the company before they will go outside the box and ask *their* managers for a bigger budget. It's a difficult conversation with the potential for conflict.

Decisions based on precedent. Managers have to consider what human resources wants (less risk), what the company wants (results), and what you want. Then they have to think about how they would respond when the next team member asks for the same thing. The easiest way to satisfy all the pressure points is to use precedents as a guide and a filter for your asks. It's easier to justify if it's been done before.

A wide range of people-management skills. There are good managers and bad managers (you'll learn from both, by the way). You'll need to have a strong understanding of your manager's strengths and weaknesses to collaborate with them effectively. Offering strength in their area of weakness is a wonderful way to complement the team and gain some momentum. For example, if your manager is a poor project manager, you can volunteer to assist, getting you closer to the strategic planning of the department.

How to Apply This Knowledge

Hate it or love it, managers are beholden to constraints that often work against the individual. If they are the company gatekeepers for budget, and they aren't usually given the budget they hope for to begin with, they may need your help to build a solid argument to go outside those parameters. Almost every significant ask I've made of my manager started with me creating a compelling argument my manager could use with their manager.

Depending on what you hope to get approved—the company's policies around change, its history, and its current goals—here are four angles from which you can approach a manager with your ask.

The experiment angle: If you're proposing a new idea you want to implement, remember how important it is to a manager to see that it's been done before. Has a precedent been set? If this is a first, you may want to pitch the idea as an experiment rather than a permanent idea. This will often get a manager over the "we haven't done it before this way" barrier.

The results angle: Your best bet of getting what you ask for is always to center it around results you have achieved because these outcomes are your greatest leverage. Consider the following starting points: a financial increase, money saved, processes streamlined, revenue generated, customer loyalty increased, new revenue stream generated, operations improved.

The level-up angle: Your manager will need to get approval from their manager for big changes or asks that have additional money attached. It's worth your time to create a strong argument that would pass muster if it went up the management chain. Focus on what's in it for the company, not what's in it for you—and show multiple paths or choices to get there.

The budget angle: If your ask requires a budget (most do), consider offering up an option of how to make the budget accommodate the new ask. Do the work to think through where the budget could be cut to make up for the new ask. Offer the solution and the logical rationale so your manager doesn't have to produce it single-handedly.

THE PROBLEM WITH HR

Human resources is the gatekeeper for all the processes that affect your career: raises, hiring, firing, promotions, performance plans, and company restructures. HR is also the quiet group in the back room working with your managers on many of your requests. Even though you may not have a lot of interaction with HR managers, it's important to understand the role they are playing in your career behind the scenes, especially as they work with your manager.

The primary goal of HR is to protect the company and contain risk. Human resources is definitely *not* a Captain America save-the-people function, like some may believe. HR isn't there to help the people get what they want. This doesn't mean that HR always chooses between loyalty to the company or to the people. The two shouldn't be mutually exclusive. But more often than I would have liked, I was containing risk for the company, and in doing so, I wasn't stacking the cards in the favor of the individual. It wasn't that I was against the people. I was just "for" the company. In that regard, human resources isn't the devil. But it's no saint, either.

At its best, HR creates programs and policies that help ensure companies are creating a culture free of discrimination and other bad behavior. They train managers to be good agents for the company. They implement pay structures that should be fair and equitable. Hopefully they create a place where people feel supported, heard, and engaged. They are also balancing all those high ideals against risk of lawsuits and making sure they help the company stay out of trouble.

TRUTH (#4)
Human resources is there to minimize risk for the company, not to fix your problems.
The trick is in knowing when they can help you and when they can hurt you. I don't know of any human resources department that wants to see an employee mistreated, but they are still serving the company first. Often that puts the individual at a disadvantage from the start.

WHAT YOU CAN EXPECT FROM HR

Clarity when it serves the company and vagueness when it doesn't. If they need to protect the company, such as making sure there is a non-compete in place, they'll put it in writing and make certain you've signed. If you accuse the company of wrongdoing, they'll often keep correspondence *out of* writing so the company isn't implicated or so they can control the narrative. It's all about minimizing risk.

Money to quietly resolve wrongdoings and avert costly legal action. They commonly use severance in exchange for a release of claims—not because they want you to land on your feet; they aren't paying it to be nice. They pay it to make perceived risk (such as a wrongful termination lawsuit) go away.

Structured programs and rules. They like programs with rules, such as pay plans or specific policies around time off or remote work. They put them in place to have a structure that can minimize lawsuits, primarily regarding discrimination. They'll push back against out-of-cycle increases or anything that doesn't fit into the box.

It sometimes feels as if HR is working against you. It's not that they don't care (because they do). It's that they care more about precedents than the individual. This is because the decisions that have been made before may become very important in lawsuits. If a company says yes to one work-from-home request but no to another, for instance, it opens the company to the risk of someone claiming they were discriminated against. But hold your judgment! Before you decide HR is a barrier, know that some of the things people love to hate about human resources, such as rules and structure, can work to your benefit—if you know how to position the ask correctly.

How to Apply This Knowledge

Here are a few tips to help you align with human resources rather than work against them:

The structured programs angle: You can use the compensation structure to work in your favor. While the default answer on raise requests is "wait until year-end reviews," there are opportunities to use the structure to benefit you. Because job descriptions change rapidly, compensation ranges are often out of date. For example, if you took on significantly more responsibility without increased pay, you need to align to the human resources sensitivities to risk. Saying you are working harder isn't compelling. But saying you have taken on six specific new responsibilities and suggesting the role may need to be rescoped to see if the pay is at the right level relative to other jobs would play into concerns about pay discrimination.

The performance plan inconsistency angle: Agents of the company (managers primarily) often don't go through the process correctly when they want to fire someone. If the company hasn't given you the right warnings, HR may become your greatest ally. You may find yourself with leverage to ask for severance to leave, in order to compensate for a manager's failure to put in place a performance plan or create clarity about what was expected of you—mistakes that create risk for the company.

The complaint/concern angle: Knowing how the company wants to control the narrative of any potential concerns regarding discrimination, you can protect yourself by putting concerns in writing with a record of delivery (email is good). This can help you establish legitimacy for your narrative and often allows you to be heard and get issues rectified faster than they would otherwise. Remember, human resources tries to control any facts that reflect poorly on the company by using very precise language to frame their position or to keep out of writing words or facts that aren't desirable.

FINAL THOUGHTS

To get something from a company, you must understand a company.

You are working with multiple tough dynamics when you are working in a company, but it doesn't have to frustrate you. See it for what it is and adjust the way you ask for what you need. Small adjustments can yield big results. It bears repeating: if you know your audience, you can know your approach.

GOVERNING PRINCIPLES OF A COMPANY

You won't take the "company" out of a company. But you can pivot your asks to align with these governing principles:

- Companies rarely make decisions that require them to spend more without getting more. Results then become your greatest currency and your greatest leverage.

- Companies aren't designed to make decisions on feelings. Your asks are more powerful when you use the language of business: numbers.
- Any ask that requires busting the budget will introduce constraints. When you show a pathway to keep your asks budget-neutral, it increases your odds of a yes.
- Program constraints and past precedents will be a driver for any decisions. Find the path that allows you to use previous decisions to your advantage.

Armed with these truths, you are much better prepared to navigate within the corporate structure. But now, you must look within and realize that it's not just the company that has problems. You do too. Next, let's explore the problems with people.

3

The Problem with
People

*Lie: I could have a much better work experience
if only my manager were a better communicator.*

*Truth: You are part of the problem.
You could have a better work experience if both
you and your manager were communicating.*

'm an equal-opportunity author. I spent the previous chapter
sharing all the ways companies operate and why they behave
the way they do. Now let's add the next layer of complication:
people. I have hired thousands of them. I have fired thousands of
them. Each of these significant life events have a host of interesting dynamics going on during the process. As an intermediary
between managers and their people, I often shake my head in dis-
belief at how poorly we all communicate, even when we are sitting
in front of each other deliberately trying to be clear.

• • •

It's easy to think that everyone else in
the workplace can't communicate, but I'm
convinced you are part of the problem.

People are flawed, especially when it comes to communication. Don't think I'm still talking about everyone else: I'm talking about you as well. I understand that your manager or coworker is flawed. However, I'm also including you and me with the whole lot. Be honest. You have, at one time or another in your career, said something like this:

- *"If I'm completely honest about what I think, I'll lose my job!"*
- *"I'm not happy with her performance, but I don't want to make this a bigger deal than it might be. I'll say nothing and see if it gets better."*
- *"My manager says he wants the truth, but there is no way I'm going to tell him how I really feel."*
- *"This idea is going to fail, but I'm not going to be the one to burst their bubble."*

At the root of such phrases is our aversion to conflict. The truth is that humans (not just managers) will naturally avoid conflict and honest dialogue when it's uncomfortable. Although employees like to blame their managers for the big disconnect, most people (managers or not) avoid difficult conversations, especially when they feel there is an element of risk. People often speak in code with careful words and unclear verbiage.

As long as an overabundance of caution dampers your candor, you will see CEOs surprised when they are let go, people confused when they are replaced or moved into new positions without warning, or the most common, work frustrations continuing to build until people give up and leave their organization.

To understand how workforce dynamics fully play out, it's important to know how people operate, especially in terms of communication. In the previous chapter, we covered some of the overarching problems with companies and how they are at the core of many lies we tell ourselves at work. In this chapter, I'll show you how people (psst—that's you!) are also part of the problem thanks to ineffective communication styles that can sink your success at work. I'll also show you how you can overcome the roadblocks you may face with company stakeholders.

Having honest conversations is the key to finding your communication success. So why is it so hard to do?

WHY IS HONEST CONVERSATION SO HARD?

In my work with thousands of clients, what I've heard boils down to this: risk. People have various ways they feel that risk shows up, but at work it usually all points to the same three concerns:

1. It will have negative career implications.
2. It will hurt the working relationship with the other person.
3. The company should already know and I shouldn't have to tell them.

Speaking up may seem like a losing proposition. But then again, it seems that during "The Great Resignation," people are finally feeling free to express how they feel and what they need in the workplace. I do believe the pendulum is swinging toward employees having greater power more than even a decade ago, when companies called all the shots.

Yet I was surprised to hear from my followers that they are more hesitant than ever to speak up in the workplace. I posed the question on social media: "Is it easier or harder than it used to be to address conflict in the workplace?" Thousands of people weighed in with comments and private email responses like these:

- "I'd rather leave than say anything. If the company doesn't know what the problem is, that's their problem. I'd rather go somewhere that 'gets it.'"
- "Everything is so polarized right now that even having an opinion is a dangerous thing. I don't dare say anything for fear of how my manager will penalize me."
- "The last thing I need is being labeled a 'disruptor' by speaking up or weighing in on difficult topics, and it would limit my career growth."
- "I'm tired. The last thing I want to do is speak up. Let me just do my job."
- "I've tried talking and nothing ever changes."
- "I'll just leave the company if I don't like it. Treat me right or I'll go."

Ninety-four percent of those that responded to my question were *less likely* to speak up in today's environment. A vast majority were likely to leave their job without speaking up first.

It's sad to me that people would rather leave a company than have a voice within it, even though I understand the "why," which ties back to feeling they have some control again. I would like to convince you that the control you are seeking is in front of you. Improving communication isn't just for the company's sake. It's for you too. While I can't guarantee that there is no risk to your career in expressing a point of view, you may be assigning more risk to speaking up than the evidence suggests.

I am convinced by watching those who are successful communicators at work that having a voice helps individuals feel they have more power and influence in their workplace. I'm also convinced there are some basics to having a good conversation when the stakes are high. You can talk with anyone about anything if you create enough safety and use facts—not emotion—to lead the conversation.

THE CONNECTION TO JOB SATISFACTION AND SPEAKING UP

You may be thinking, "My manager isn't like that. My manager would fire me if I spoke up." We like to think the real problem is that there are penalties attached to speaking up. No doubt when it's done the wrong way, that can be true. It takes only one bad experience to convince an individual that they should never speak up. But likewise, a good experience can fuel courage for more good dialogue, which leads to greater participation, which leads to work satisfaction.

The conversations you are avoiding are the exact conversations that can give you back a sense of control at work.

Does it surprise you that the thing many individuals avoid—honest communication—is the key to feeling a sense of control and greater engagement? It isn't just that getting something off your chest feels good. Sharing your opinion and feeling you have a voice makes you more engaged and involved at work, which correlates directly to work satisfaction. Elizabeth McCune is director of employee listening systems and culture measurement at Microsoft. She coauthored an *MIT Sloan Management Review* article entitled "When Employees Speak Up, Companies Win" on the impact of the employee voice.[1] Roughly six thousand Microsoft employees were asked how often they spoke up to their managers about fifteen topics including their jobs, culture, strategy of the company, and work-life balance alternatives available to them. Not surprisingly, few chose to share often with their managers. Over 47 percent said they speak up on five or fewer topics related to their jobs. Only 13.6 percent said they were willing to regularly speak up on ten or more topics.

You may be nodding your head in agreement. In fact, almost 100 percent of employees I show these numbers to say they find it incredibly uncomfortable to speak up at all, and many would rather leave if they were unhappy rather than risk a conversation that goes sideways. If you are one of those people, consider the most important part of the data: the indisputable link to speaking up and employee engagement.

Only a small group of employees dared to speak up on a regular basis. Those who did had a vastly different employee experience: Those who voiced their views on at least fifteen topics were 92 percent more likely to want to stay with the company even if offered a comparable position elsewhere. And 95 percent of these said their company was a great place to work.

On the flip side, those who didn't speak up at all or who shared opinions only occasionally were only 60 percent likely to stay with the company—a substantial drop. Being able to voice one's views contributed to the overall connection with not only their department but also the company as a whole.

These numbers also closely align with the likelihood of employees recommending their company to prospective job seekers, as well as the level of excitement they feel about their jobs. The more an employee is engaged in active and open communication (even if it results in some uncomfortable conversations), the more likely they are to feel connected to the company's goals and mission—and the more likely they are to stay.

Those actively engaged in communication on a multitude of topics were 95 percent more likely both to recommend their company to others and feel excitement about their work. That's more than a 30-point jump in overall job satisfaction and enthusiasm over those who do not speak up.

If you are waiting to feel that you are a part of a company by getting the things the company provides—such as pay, benefits, and flexible work hours—you may still find yourself feeling empty at the end of the day. If you are making a fair (or fair-enough) wage for your work, feeling that you belong and that your voice makes a difference is a far more potent tool for satisfaction than external offerings.

STOP AND THINK . . .

- How many times have you shared your views where you work?
- Is it possible that your lack of communication is contributing to a lack of engagement?

If you are like many of the people I work with, part of what may be keeping you from speaking up could be more than simple discomfort with rocking the boat. I have found with my clients, and particularly those in Gen Z, there are questions about the right way to communicate and how to navigate being honest versus being careful. Not knowing leads people to talk a big game about the clear conversation that took place, but upon peeling it back, everyone is talking around the edges of the issue without ever being clear. I call it a "halfway conversation."

Let's take a look at some of the most common ways employees miscommunicate at work.

HALFWAY CONVERSATIONS

If you start watching around you, you'll see that halfway conversations are the hallmark of the workplace. People will often intend to have a clear conversation but water down their words, share only partial truths, and hope the other person gets the gist of what they are saying. We are polite with one another. We smile and nod. We work through our agendas and appear as though we are all on the same page. But most often, nothing could be further from the truth. The conversations going on in our own heads and with our close colleagues are nothing like the ones playing out at work every day.

Thinking you are clear in a halfway conversation is the first gap you need to address.

If your conversations are only halfway to the truth,
expect the other party will walk away understanding
only as much as a quarter of the problem.

This isn't found only in meetings where people talk past each other (although that's a great place to see halfway conversations). It happens in every critical career interaction—performance plans, career growth and pay discussions, strategy or work sessions, and interviews. The truth is, individuals are more skilled than ever at pretending we are communicating when we clearly are not.

We all share in this communication problem—even you. Do you recognize yourself in any of the following workplace conversations? It's easier to read between the lines and grasp what is really being said when we see it in writing, but it's harder to notice in the moments when you are having conversations that sow the seeds of dissatisfaction at work.

Team Meetings

Manager: *I'd love to hear any feedback you have about these goals for our department. I think they can make a real difference to the business, but you are all closer to the problems and may have additional ideas.*

Employees during meeting: *(Crickets)*

Employees after meeting: *Can you believe how disconnected our manager is from reality? I guess he'll learn what a bad idea that is when it fails.*

One-on-One Meetings

Manager: *How are you liking your job? Is there anything I could do better for you?*

Employee to Manager: *I'm still learning parts of the job, but it's coming along. I know I can come to you if I need anything.*

Employee to Friend: *Are they serious? It's the worst job I've ever had. Where is all the training I was promised? My manager hasn't done more than give me a desk and computer.*

Promotions/Demotions

Hiring Manager to Employee: *You were close to getting the job, but we ultimately decided on one of the other candidates.*

Hiring Manager to HR: *I don't think he would work for the job. He has a reputation for not working well with other departments.*

Hiring Manager to Employee: *Keep applying! Another candidate with more experience got the role, but it's only a matter of time before you get the promotion.*

Leaving a Job

Manager: *Hannah is one of my best people and I can't afford to lose her. I gave her a bigger raise than others on the team and she knows she's a top performer. I had no idea she was unhappy.*

Hannah in Exit Interview: *I took on Jennie's job when she left. It was supposed to be temporary. I have been working fifty-hour workweeks and only got a 5 percent raise. Barely above cost of living. I've asked my manager to look at my pay, but she never does anything about it.*

Recruiting

Recruiter: *This company is a family. We really support and help one another.*

Employee: *By "family," they meant they play favorites, yell at each other all the time, and are always arguing about money.*

When company leadership leads with halfway conversations, managers tend to follow that lead, and this vague and indirect style can filter down to employees. This does a couple of things. First, it grows frustration ("What does leadership *really* mean? I feel like they aren't being honest with me"). It can also influence how you interact with managers because, over time, employees often mirror the communication style of their leadership. So, let's turn the lens on you. Because, believe it or not, other people have to read between your lines as well.

THE POWER OF THE REFRAME

It's not only our conversations that are halfway. Sometimes the beliefs we adopt are also only half of the truth. This idea of missing what's really going on is critical as you begin to assess all the proof points around you about whether your workplace is somewhere you can succeed. Be open to revising your beliefs. You are basing your workplace story on what you see, but just like an iceberg in the ocean, there may be more to it than what is showing above the surface.

You've probably heard the story of the "Three Little Pigs." At first glance, it's a simple fable about the merits of hard work and doing the right job the first time. Walt Disney's 1933 version of the folktale is considered one of the most successful short animated films of all time and is preserved in the National Film Registry by the Library of Congress for its cultural and historic significance. A folktale about pigs that is culturally significant? You see, the film wasn't really about pigs and houses and sticks at all. Instead, it was a metaphor for the nation as its people grappled with the downturn of the Great Depression and their fight for survival. The real message was about overcoming the adversities brought about by the Depression "beating down the doors" of everyday life and security. Deep stuff.

Disney reframed the "Three Little Pigs." And likewise, I want to positively reframe your work beliefs from lies to truths. This mighty game changer will give you a better starting place from which to navigate. It will help you have a good relationship with your manager, get results that translate into pay or promotions, minimize work burnout, and help you be seen as a top performer.

I want you to see the workplace through fresh eyes: instead of looking to the company and hoping you can find one that provides the right setting, the right culture, or the right rules and processes, I want you to understand the levers you can pull to enjoy and accelerate your career.

You don't reclaim your workplace satisfaction by hopping from one job to another. You also don't have to just grin and bear it when you are miserable.

How to Reframe Your Thinking About Work

I don't want anyone to gloss over the value of a good reframe. In its simplest terms, a reframe means to change the way you think.

> *To reframe something, one must make*
> *a deliberate shift in the way one sees things,*
> *even though the facts remain the same.*

Reframing, especially when it's a positive reframe, moves an individual from a powerless position of being a victim (in this case of the corporate world) to being able to see how to influence, change, respond, or promote new actions or ideas. Reframing asks you to question your current beliefs and reactions to those beliefs and replace those thought patterns with a better perspective. Bottom line: it's about being aware of and changing your thought habits.

The facts don't change in a situation. Your story or rationale of why the facts exist is what needs to broaden. If you are steeped in negative beliefs about your company or its managers, everything you experience will support this point of view. If you walk around thinking companies are going to do you wrong, you will find evidence to support it. Likewise, if you think managers are out for themselves and don't care about you, that's the experience you will get.

As I collaborate with clients on reframing their beliefs, the first comment I often get is, "You're trying to manipulate the facts."

My answer is this: **"You can't manipulate the facts. But we mistakenly mix up our facts with our framing. Your framing is the story you tell about the facts. Doing that is nothing more than manipulating the conclusion you draw from the facts to support your own beliefs."**

Being aware that you are manipulating the facts to support your beliefs is the first step in creating a powerful reframe. The stories you tell have dramatic impacts on the outcomes you get. Reframes create new possibilities. They expand the potential outcomes. Take a look at this example and see how a different path can emerge with a reframe.

CASE STUDY: I NEVER GET THE PROMOTION

The indisputable fact: I have applied for several promotions, and I am never hired.

How the employee frames it:

- The company politics are getting in the way—I don't have the right friends in the right places.
- The manager has never liked me and is holding me back.
- There is no interest in hiring a woman in this male-dominated industry.
- I'm in a company that doesn't want doers; they want smooth talkers.
- The decision was made before I ever got in the mix.

The likely outcome: This person will choose to leave the company soon. When she does, the story will be that this is a company that doesn't support personal growth or value diversity.

A reframe: Identify a different set of reasons why the individual might not have gotten the job. This list should assume the company/manager has good intent rather than bad intent. Note that if you tend to go negative on your framing, it may take some concentration to produce a new list that looks more like this:

- There may be a perceived personal shortcoming I don't understand in my skill set.
- I may not have expressed my value proposition for the role with clarity.
- Another candidate may have expressed an interest in this role months ago, and the manager is more familiar with their results and their capabilities.
- My manager may feel I'm not ready for the promotion or feel I'm optimally placed today.

- I am considered a strong talent and the company has another position in mind, or it's been discussed that I would be the one they would choose for the next promotion.

Which is correct? The first list or the second? The answer is that we don't know for sure. The only thing we know is there could be more reasons, some of which are less adversarial. When the framing includes a broader list of possibilities, it also brings with it a different set of actions to gather more facts that can shed light on where the truth really lies.

The better potential outcome: With a different set of possibilities to explain why you didn't get the job, the next logical steps may look something like this:

- Have a sit-down conversation with the hiring manager to understand why a different selection was made and seek honest feedback.
- Develop a career growth plan with your current manager to map out next steps and solicit their support.
- Attend a coaching session to fine-tune your value proposition and a plan to better communicate it, whether in a resume or an interview.
- Participate in a 360-degree feedback strategy (see page 78) to better understand how you are perceived in the organization.

Reframing may be one of the hardest principles to put into practice because in our culture we have difficulty seeing different perspectives outside of our own.

How Badly Are You in Need of a Reframe?

Let's do an exercise together to see what your framing currently looks like, so you have a baseline from which to explore the lies and truths in the coming chapters. Answer these questions honestly, and don't overthink them. You are not being graded on this exercise. It is intended to give you a starting point—a way to know which chapters you may need to pay the most attention to in order to give you the biggest boost to your own personal reframe.

My Beliefs About the Workplace

Write down your score from 1 to 10 on each statement, with a 10 meaning you strongly agree with the statement.

- "If I push to improve my work-life balance, _____
my job will be in jeopardy."
- "If I work harder, the company will eventually _____
see it and reward me."
- "Only those who play the politics game can get _____
a promotion."
- "If I have the right title, I can be more _____
strategic."
- "If there is a problem with my performance, _____
I will know about it."
- "If I push back and create conflict, it will hurt _____
my career."
- "If I get overloaded at work, the best approach is _____
to push hard to get caught up."
- "If I've been a great performer, I should be able _____
to get a solid raise at annual appraisals."
- "If I had a clearer understanding of my job _____
description, I could be more successful."

- "There's not much I can do about company   _____
  burnout other than change jobs."

SCORING	
90-100 POINTS VICTIM/MARTYR	*I am just another victim of a broken corporate world, where people get used up and spit out.*
70-90 POINTS SOMEBODY ELSE'S FAULT	*Companies care only about some people, and unless I "play the game," I can't win.*
60-70 POINTS PASSIVE	*The corporate world is a mystery to me. I keep my head down, stay out of trouble, and hope for the best.*
40-60 POINTS TESTING WATERS	*The corporate world stretches me, but there is a place for me if I do the work.*
0-40 POINTS PROACTIVE	*While the path isn't perfectly clear in companies, I have confidence I can make important contributions.*

Would it surprise you to know that every single one of these statements is false—or at least mostly false? The higher your cumulative number, the tougher it will be for you to reframe your beliefs, because it's a reflection of how you have framed the workforce already. The higher your number, the more skeptical you may be as to whether the company or anything you do can create a positive career experience. I don't disagree that your experiences have shaped your views, but I may disagree with your *reasons* for why these experiences occurred. If this is the case, know that the work ahead will be harder for you than for someone with a lower score because you will be looking for negative points that reinforce your beliefs.

FINAL THOUGHTS

Now that you've explored the problems with companies and the problems with people and learned how to reframe your thinking, let's start digging into each lie one at a time and see how you got here so you can reframe them as the truths they really are.

In a perfect world, it would be easy to say that companies have to change (and I do hope that companies will change their model in the future). But this book is about the individual—*you*—and how you interact within the workplace to have a better experience. Like it or not, the workplace is a less than perfect environment paired with less than perfect individuals (and yes, that includes you).

4

Lies About Performance

*Lie: If there is a problem with me that could
be career-limiting, I will know about it.*

Truth: You won't know about it.

I was in the room when the CEO was fired.

I thought I was attending an early-morning meeting to finalize some equity grants for the team. I stepped into the conference room where the CEO and the head of our board were waiting. Ten minutes later, the CEO was being ushered from the building, and my work world had shifted.

The next half hour was one of the most interesting experiences of my career. I was led into a conference room where I was introduced to the new CEO. He told me we would be losing over half of our executive team. He then threw an unexpected wrench into the discussion. He asked if I wanted to be one of the executives who left the company or if I wanted to stay.

In that moment I realized two things: First, I knew there were some concerns following a failed merger/acquisition. It's not as though anyone sat around talking about the CEO, but because we worked together every day, we knew his shortcomings as well as his strengths. While the firing seemed to surprise the CEO, it didn't surprise those who worked closely with him.

The second surprise was my realization that I didn't have an accurate take on how I was viewed in the organization. Of course it made sense that I could see the CEO bomb coming. But the possibility that I could be on the short list? That was a shock.

There is nothing as humbling as realizing your blind spot limited your view of the one person you thought you knew best of all—yourself.

Not knowing whether this was an ending or a new beginning was a sobering moment. As we spoke, the new CEO gave me feedback about some of my own strengths and weaknesses, and what needed to happen for me to have a good experience under his leadership.

What I learned about how I was perceived blew me away. I was viewed as negative, particularly toward the sales department, the lifeblood of our company. While this new CEO thankfully assumed good intent on my part, acknowledging there were reasons to be frustrated, he helped me understand that without teams that could partner well, our organization wouldn't work. His ask was very specific to me: Did I think I could change? He went on to say that if I couldn't, then I would be a detractor to the unity he needed to create for us to get back on track. He left me with a decision to make: whether I wanted to stay and make changes or leave with the other half of the executive team.

Talk about clarity. Without it, I never could have gone on to have several successful years of tremendous career growth under this new CEO.

This experience led to an epiphany. From the CEO to the most entry-level person in a company, we do not know how we are perceived. You don't have a fully accurate view of how the executives, your manager, and your coworkers experience you. It was only after I had this eye-opening experience that I realized this critical principle. I was the head of human resources! I was the leader who was supposed to be the most plugged in to the company's people and performance! And I was blind to my own weak spots.

The feedback the new CEO gave me was critical to my future success. When I stopped to think about my own experience that day, I couldn't help but wonder about every employee who had ever been let go or who had not gotten the position or promotion they wanted. All those individuals were missing critical insights into how they were perceived. Each knew a portion of the truth, but not the whole truth. I began to catalog in my mind all the data I had amassed through countless hirings, firings, restructures, and reductions. I had been privy to thousands of defining moments—the best and worst career days of many people's lives. One thing became very clear: your manager's perception is reality.

I wish I had better news for you. But you're better off knowing it now so you aren't caught flat-footed later.

Every single piece of feedback you hear about yourself,
whether neutral or negative, needs to be taken seriously.
It's a watered-down version of how you are actually perceived.

There is a silver lining in all this. You are not destined to be stuck in this place of "unknowing" forever unless you decide that's what you want for yourself. Watching those who are brave enough to seek clarity and make quick course corrections regularly has convinced me it's a better plan, despite the discomfort.

You can learn to notice the subtle feedback clues from managers and coworkers, which give you an opportunity to proactively address your perception. You don't have to wait on the company and hope you get the feedback you need. You might not know how you are perceived all the time, but you can create the conditions for greater truth-telling, and you can own the process of getting feedback, which allows for constant refinement and small adjustments that can make a massive difference in your career.

When I speak to groups of employees, I routinely ask the question, "How many of you want to know how you are viewed in your organizations?" to which almost every hand in the room goes up. Then I ask a follow-up question, "How many of you feel you have an accurate view of how you are perceived?" Without fail, only a fraction of the hands go up. The gap between wanting the truth and getting the truth is significant.

Most people have been in the workforce long enough to have either experienced an unexpected termination, a lower-than-expected performance review, mixed messages from a manager, or a lack of career growth with no honest explanation. From entry-level employee to CEO, people often don't know where they stand. A large majority of people simply assume this is a fact they must accept.

You may be directionally correct with how you are perceived, especially if you have a manager who is a strong communicator. But there is a difference between knowing how your manager and coworkers generally perceive you and knowing the full truth.

Being only directionally correct about how you are perceived versus having clarity can be the difference between succeeding and failing.

In this chapter, I'll explain how you're missing your own performance blind spots and how you can learn to pay closer attention to company stakeholders and set yourself up for success.

DECODING YOUR MANAGER

The best place to begin understanding how you are perceived is with your manager. Their perception of you is the most important one to understand because they have the potential to be your greatest advocate or your greatest barrier. If problems are emerging, they may say something at your performance appraisal or drop clues verbally in their day-to-day interactions with you.

But how do you improve yourself if you don't even know your blind spots? There are two ways I've seen that can help you get closer to the truth. First, you can just get better at reading between the lines when your manager communicates. In other words, you learn to read their halfway conversations. Second, you can pay attention to their behavior with you. There are subtle clues that managers tend to give when there is an emerging problem. It's not a perfectly accurate or fail-proof list, because managers sometimes change up their work style for other reasons. But just like when a rainstorm is coming and you can smell it in the air, I've seen what unresolved performance concerns look like in a manager, and it's worth paying attention.

Before all the managers reading this book are offended, I have used these examples as an illustrative target because it's easy to see the disconnect between when we think we have been clear about performance and what honest feedback looks like. There are some wonderful managers out there who could teach a master class on performance communication. Not saying what we mean isn't solely a manager problem. It's a people problem, which we just reviewed in the previous chapter. For now, let's focus on you and your manager, how performance disconnects show up, and how you can decode the information that comes at you.

WATCH FOR MANAGEMENT BEHAVIOR CHANGES

Let's first focus on your manager's behavior. If trouble is on the horizon, your manager is likely to do the following:

Reduce or increase oversight. Either they are behaving like a micromanager and checking over all of your work, or they suddenly seem to disengage.

Request time tracking of your day. There are a few instances when this is a legitimate request such as a project manager who must track time against billable hours, but if you are in a role that hasn't previously required you to track time, it usually has its roots in a concern about how you are using your time.

Start following up every meeting with an email. This is an often-used tactic in cooperation with HR to begin creating a paper trail of expectations versus results and clarity around job expectations. While it is also a good practice to get people on the same page and doesn't have to be nefarious, few busy managers naturally incorporate a process that includes this level of follow-through.

Continually request rework. Are you being asked to redo proposals, reports, and presentations, or given feedback that your work isn't quite right? While it could be some micromanaging, if it's a new pattern change for your manager, pay attention.

Ask other team members to pick up work you used to handle.
Often a vote of no confidence shows up as a shift of one person's
work to a more trusted team member.

Cancel meetings with you. If you are finding that it's increas-
ingly rare to get face time with your manager, and this is a new
development, it could spell trouble.

Interact less with you during meetings. If you used to be
called on for ideas frequently and now your manager doesn't make
eye contact or include you in the conversation as often, there may
be an issue brewing.

If these look familiar to you, then it's time to have a frank discussion with your manager. While I just spent several minutes convincing you it's hard to get accurate information, know that the
goal of this conversation is intended to get you one step closer to a
more accurate understanding of how you are viewed. It isn't going
to get you all the way there unless you have already built a great
partnership with your manager. But perfection isn't the goal. Even
getting 10 percent more clarity is a step in the right direction.

Let's cover some tricks about how to have a conversation that
gets you closer to the truth with as little risk as possible to your
career. (The structure of this conversation is discussed in more
depth on page 64.)

Manager Script: What's Really Going On?

For illustrative purposes, I've used an example from
the list of management behavior changes. For your situation, use your own examples. Here are some things you can say
in response to your manager's actions or words:

CREATE SAFETY

I want you to be able to count on me and be a valuable part of this team. I love working here and it's important to me that you can trust the work I do.

PROBLEM SUMMARY

I have noticed some differences in our interaction lately, and it leaves me feeling worried. There may be nothing to it at all, but I'd like to really find out if that is the case.

WHAT I EXPECTED

In the past, you have given me assignments with a lot of autonomy to get them across the finish line. When I complete them, I may get a small suggestion or edit, but rarely do you ask for big changes. I've also been tapped by you on a pretty regular basis for extra assignments, especially those around the customer experience initiatives.

WHAT I OBSERVED

I have noticed that in the last three assignments you've given me, you have made significant changes to the wording or the approach. Where there used to be minor edits, now much of what I'm completing has to be redone, and it feels like I'm not meeting your expectations in some way. As well, I have seen you give Lauren two assignments that I would normally take on.

THE HANDOFF

Rather than guessing or reading too much into things, I want to understand your perspective. It feels like there may be a concern about my performance we should talk about. I want to give you permission to be 100 percent honest with me. It's the only way I can really grow and learn.

Am I reading this right?

or

Is that what you intended?

or

Do you see it differently?

Note that all three of these closing questions assume good intent and leave space for positive dialogue to continue. See more on page 128.

PAY ATTENTION TO COMMUNICATION CLUES

As a lifetime HR professional, here's the one thing I can predict with certainty: A manager is going to come to me when they want to fire somebody. I will say, "Do they know it's coming?" to which the manager will say, "There's no way they don't know it's coming."

What I know for sure: They don't know what's coming.

It's a frequent occurrence to have a disconnect between what a manager says and what they think they have conveyed. Their language is often watered down or they have a halfway conversation that leaves out important clarifying details. Instead of direct feedback with examples, it's carefully worded and contains veiled comments. When I peel back the actual conversations between management and the soon-to-be fired, what I will inevitably learn is that a conflict has been building for some time.

Let's dissect a typical conversation that a manager who wants to fire someone has with human resources.

The situation: A manager comes to me and says an employee has poor-quality work and it must be redone over and over. They are ready to fire the employee, who hasn't made the required changes. They will often say, "I've given them feedback about this many times." When pressed to get more specific, this is the sum of the feedback that individual has received:

- *"I need you to double-check your work to make sure there aren't errors."*
- *"Will you redo this document? I noticed some errors on it. Watch more closely in the future."*
- *"I found another mistake. You can't miss these."*

The manager may feel that they have delivered adequate feedback. However, if I were the employee in question and read these comments, I would not view myself as on the verge of being fired! It sounds more like a passing comment or sound advice rather than a performance plan. I view these comments as the starting point of a conversation, but many managers use them as the entire conversation and rely on the employee to read between the lines.

I often ask managers, "If the only feedback you received before getting fired was what you just told me you shared, would you have felt you had been adequately coached and the only remaining option was termination?" This inevitably leads to a more complete conversation and coaching with the employee.

What the employee *should* have heard instead of half-truths and veiled criticism is a manager discussion like this:

I have noticed that many of the finished work products you are turning in have more errors than I would expect to see. I would expect an error or two in the formatting, for example. But in the past five assignments, I've noticed there are twenty or more errors. I want to review one of these with you to show you what I'm seeing.

When you make these mistakes, it makes our department look unprofessional and leaves a bad impression for our clients. Also, because someone has to look over your work, it is creating a bigger workload for another team member. We are all prepared to help one another, but when it becomes a regular add to their job, it doesn't create a positive work dynamic.

Is there something going on I don't understand? What could prevent this from happening again? How can I help?

This communication gap is unbelievably common. There are some red flags to look for that are common manager attempts to give a "light" version of feedback. More times than not, these are early clues for knowing where you stand. If that's the case, don't view these as bad news, because they are an incredible gift to you!

The following clues can help you adjust your behaviors and work style if necessary. It's like a breadcrumb your manager leaves that allows you to ask clarifying questions and get clear with each other on expectations and performance.

These phrases aren't always an indication of a problem, but it's worth clarifying if you hear one of them when speaking with your manager:

MANAGER CLUES

- "I want to clarify your role." (This often means, "I'm not getting what I expect from you.")
- "I'd like to understand better your project load." (This often means, "Your output is lower than I expect to see.")
- "I'll send an email to make sure we are on the same page." (This often means, "We've had some miscommunication in the past.")
- "I thought I clarified . . ." (This often means, "You didn't meet my expectations in some way.")
- "It caught me off guard when you . . ." (This often means, "You did not meet one or more of my expectations.")
- "Didn't we already agree?" (This often means, "Why did you change direction without checking in?")
- "I'm not sure we are on the same page." (This often means, "I'm concerned about your approach or see risk in the potential outcome.")
- "I'd like to carve out some time to talk to you about a few things." (This often means, "I need to have a difficult conversation with you.")

In summary, your manager will be far from perfect in addressing those areas that you may need to improve, but by paying attention to the clues they give, you have an opportunity to drive clarifying dialogue early. You'll find it easier to start early than to wait until it's more serious (more on how to respond to a written or verbal warning is in chapter 7, "Getting Comfortable with Conflict").

There is one additional area where you will have another opportunity to get clear: the universally hated performance review. A tool designed to give you truthful feedback should be something you can trust, yet it can leave a person more confused than ever. These scores, which are supposed to be the truest assessment of how a person is doing, are notoriously unhelpful and can be one of the most difficult to interpret. Despite the problems with reviews, they're a perfect opportunity to get clarity—if you ask the right questions.

GET CLEAR ON PERFORMANCE REVIEWS

Comedian Brian Regan has a routine about going to the emergency room. During check-in, he is asked to provide a number between 1 and 10 corresponding to his pain level. When the nurse asks him to give his number, he gives a "7" and quickly realizes by the nurse's lackluster response that the number isn't going to get him the attention he needs. He quickly corrects and gives the nurse a new pain number. He says emphatically, "It's an 8!" and

Cullyn Cowell

immediately the team springs into action. To all the other patients who come into the emergency room, he yells, "Say it's an 8!"

Performance reviews are similar. You get no love if you "meet expectations" (which is usually a "3" for many companies on their 1 to 5 scale). In the case of a performance review, "Say it's a 4!" corresponds to being a top performer. The problem is most companies ask their managers to adhere to a bell curve, so the majority of reviews come back as "meets expectations."

I don't trust the "meets expectations" bucket and you shouldn't either (see figure 1). It tells you very little about your true potential and performance. It's a "thanks for the effort" without much clarity about whether you are doing just good enough or something better than that. On the other hand, if you are an "exceeds expectations" employee, it's clear you are in a special club and a top performer. Managers love these conversations because they get to share good news.

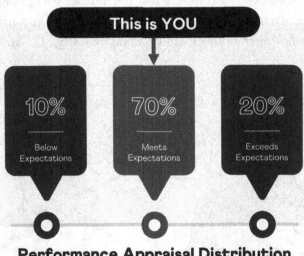

Ahmed Khalid Khan

FIGURE 1

If your manager hasn't indicated you are a top performer,
you aren't one. Top talent gets told they are top talent.

Ouch. That may sting to hear. You may be a hard-enough or good-enough worker, but that is different from being labeled a top performer. There are conversations happening behind closed doors all the time about this elite group. Many companies have private talent management meetings where they further categorize individuals. These rankings drive which people will get extra time and attention to hopefully accelerate them into the next role.

For those individuals who are in the elite group, companies provide opportunities in the form of extra training, mentoring, or exposure to experiences that can widen an employee's view of the company outside of their department. It's not provided with a lot of public fanfare or announcements, because the last thing a company wants to do is make the other 80 percent feel "less than." But make no mistake—an elite top performer will know they are one. These individuals are likely to have opportunities handed to them that others do not. Sometimes it's in the form of bonuses, equity grants, or base pay increases. More often, it's in the form of a talent management plan to accelerate their growth.

If you didn't realize all this is going on under your nose, you wouldn't be the first. Even some of the executives aren't aware when human resources is working on talent-ranking exercises for the board, for example. But just because you don't know about all this doesn't mean you are destined to get the short end of the stick.

DIRECTING YOUR OWN DEVELOPMENT PLAN

It may seem farfetched, but you can ask for the same experiences, exposures, and training that your elite peers are getting. It may not include the pay increases yet, but don't worry. Those will come after you begin to get top performer results.

In fact, offering up suggestions to assist in your growth will likely lead your manager to sigh with relief! Your manager will welcome your input about how to develop you. Adding to your manager's delight is that many of the ways to give you experiences and exposure also lighten their load. It's a double-whammy gain for a manager. I've seen many average performers blow past their high-potential peers by self-directing their own development plan to their manager. It's a hard gig for a manager to run the department, balance the budget, and be attuned enough with each person to actively think about development outside of annual reviews.

Managers love when their team members write the script for what they need.

Most talent management plans are made up of two critical elements. The first element is providing exposure and experiences that widen one's depth and visibility within the organization. If an individual gets to work on a cross-functional team, for example, they understand better how the company works! If they have visibility into executive meetings, they are learning how decisions are made and how to better frame ideas for executive support. A promotability plan is all about better understanding the ecosystem of a company. A secondary benefit is that this exposure to other people and parts of the company, particularly when you are allowed to showcase your capabilities, makes you a known entity for future promotions.

The hardest part of a self-directed plan is knowing what to ask for. You may not know exactly what you need, but a good place to start is asking for opportunities to expand others' visibility to you, and also expand your visibility to others in the company.

TALENT MANAGEMENT MENU

The following list contains some of the most common elements to a talent management promotion plan. Often managers will have help from human resources to design a custom plan, but you can easily create your own and ask for your manager to help support it.

Experiences

- Manage a department or cross-functional project.
- Develop a department dashboard to measure traction on key metrics.
- Give a presentation or proposal in an executive meeting.
- Volunteer to assist your manager with an initiative or a priority that is losing steam.
- Spearhead an employee resource group (known as an ERG) for the company.
- Manage a team or department meeting for your manager when they are absent.

Exposure

- Sit in on a leadership meeting to see how decisions are made and the cadence of conversations.
- Attend a partner meeting or company-sponsored conference you wouldn't normally attend.
- Spend the day shadowing sales or another department you need to collaborate with frequently.

- If the company is public, listen to the quarterly reporting and follow up by asking leaders questions about areas of interest.

Training

- Take a course on using data and analytics—every job needs this skill.
- Get proficient on building intermediate-level presentations.
- Become a better project manager (consider PMP Certification or Google certificate).
- Take a master class on how to negotiate.
- Attend an internal training course outside of compliance courses to learn about other parts of the company.

The second element to a talent management plan is mentoring. However, this is a frequently misunderstood term. It isn't as difficult as people think and it certainly isn't about walking around and asking people, "Will you be my mentor?" It is available to everyone once you realize all the ways it can be structured. At its core, it's nothing more than finding a trusted business professional that you can look to for expertise or feedback or to otherwise connect you to the experiences you need to grow. It certainly doesn't need to be one person—it can by many. Nor does it need to be a formal relationship.

The best form of mentoring is to see excellence modeled.
No talent management initiative or manager needs to
intervene for you to find people you can watch closely.

One of the easiest ways to learn from others is to watch those in your organization who are skilled in an area. Study them doing "that thing" they do well. Maybe they are skilled in running meetings. Or they are a manager who creates proposals that always make their way across the finish line. Wherever excellence exists, find it and watch it. Then, when it's your turn to do "that thing," ask the expert some questions. "What do you think the key is to a great proposal and what do you attribute to your high success rate for getting a yes on yours?" I don't know anyone in the workplace who would turn down a request to talk more about why they are good at what they do.

Consider finding experts you can observe and learn from in these critical areas:

MENTOR SKILLS CHECKLIST

- Making compelling proposals
- Diffusing conflict
- Creating strong partnerships across departments
- Leading an effective meeting
- Creating compelling dashboards or storytelling through metrics
- Aligning teams through project management
- Leading teams and increasing employee engagement

If you reframe your view of mentoring from a formal mentor to instead finding the experts to watch and learn from, there is no limit to the number of mentors guiding you at any given time. This, combined with making active asks to gain experience outside of your current role or department, will mimic a top-talent development plan that is every bit as strong as any company- or manager-directed plan.

DOUBLE DOWN ON SELF-DIRECTED FEEDBACK

If you want to accelerate your growth, double down on getting feedback. The biggest problem with waiting on your manager to drive the process is that your manager's first priority isn't you. The only one whose priority is you is *you*. Yet you are the one who benefits the most by getting clear feedback.

Far better than waiting on your manager or a company process is to own the feedback process yourself. The idea of proactively asking how not only your manager but also others in the organization perceive you may not sound particularly comfortable. But if there is a theme throughout this book, it is the importance of getting uncomfortable: whether it's by speaking up, hitting conflict head-on, asking for what you need, or asking for more regular feedback.

My advice earlier was to listen for feedback breadcrumbs; that's a tool you can use every single day. But when it comes to accelerating your momentum, you need to do more than just listen carefully—you have to seek feedback out and create the conditions for greater truth-telling. True, it may be easier to stick your head in the sand and wait until you're forced to learn what people really think of you. Most individuals wait until the company deems that it is appraisal time, and even then, I think if most of us were given the choice, we would skip it altogether. At that pace, you're missing an opportunity to make course corrections all throughout the year.

Walk through the front door of feedback
instead of waiting for it to come to you.

Yes, it takes nerves of steel to ask for information that might not be what you want to hear. It's about as fun as going to the dentist. It is uncomfortable. But frequent feedback, while difficult at first, will become more familiar to you as you receive it. You'll begin to have the following realizations:

- Feedback is unsettling until it becomes more familiar.
- When feedback becomes familiar, it begins to feel safe.
- Feedback that feels safe begins to be more like coaching.

SELF-DIRECTED FEEDBACK OPTIONS

While there are many different ways to seek input, I've found there are several that create the conditions for great personal insights. The beauty of these ideas is that any individual can start at any time in a career and yield great benefits! They don't require permission. They don't require training. The only thing required is taking a deep breath and diving in.

Quick Validate

A quick validate is nothing more than a question or two to quickly ascertain if you are on track. It's a technique that is intended to be light (rather than a heavy conversation). As such, it's done on the fly and requires no formality.

In fact, the one rule of a quick validate is that you don't schedule a meeting for it. This isn't the place for a long conversation; it's not the time to get defensive. The purpose is to listen and make quick adjustments. Organic by nature, it's intended to check direction, confirm alignment, and affirm ideal work style. Getting this type of feedback is a risk-free proposition.

There is hardly an easier way to validate approach or direction than to tag on a quick question at the end of a conversation. Here are some questions you can use:

QUICK VALIDATE PHRASES

- *"I want to confirm what I'm hearing . . ."*
- *"It sounds like what you are expecting is . . ."*
- *"Let me repeat back what I understand to be our plan. Have I got it right?"*
- *"What would be the best outcome in your view?"*
- *"Is there anything you are seeing that worries you?"*
- *"Any recommendations on adjustments?"*
- *"What advice would you give me on this?"*
- *"How do you feel X went? I'd value your feedback."*
- *"What are your observations about X?"*

Remember: you work *with* people, not just *for* people. How your colleagues feel about and respond to you at work matters, so getting feedback from them, too, is valuable for your career growth mindset.

Feedback Four-Pack Plan

There is a process called 360-degree feedback in which you get perspectives from multiple people to create a balanced picture of how others view you. Typically, you get perspectives from those

LIES ABOUT PERFORMANCE **79**

who report to you, those to whom you report, and those who have worked with you in a cross-functional capacity.

I'm a big believer in getting balanced feedback from more than one source. Your manager may be the most important relationship you have at work, but the way you work is defined by more than one relationship. Your ability to manage down is every bit as important as your ability to manage up. Managing across into other departments is also critical; it's one of the career growth markers you'll learn about in the chapter about promotability.

I learned I was a micromanager from team feedback in a 360 review. That feedback would never have shown up from my leaders or peers because, in part, I don't manage my peers. They saw only the side of me that interacted in executive meetings, and they saw the outcomes of my department, which were strong. They didn't see the ineffective way that some team members felt I got those results.

My recommendation is to create your own 360 feedback plan through something I call the Feedback Four-Pack. It's a mini version of a complete 360 review, with four people weighing in on their perceptions two or three times per year. These sessions should be brief, no more than twenty minutes. You'll get the best results if you structure the feedback in a brief conversation with four simple questions designed to allow the feedback to surface quickly.

Pick Your Four-Pack

1. Your manager (this one is nonnegotiable)
2. A coworker with whom you have a positive relationship
3. A coworker with whom you have a neutral relationship
4. A manager outside of your department who would have a view of your work

FEEDBACK SCRIPT

I am a believer in learning how others perceive me and doing check-ins with people who have an opportunity to see my work often. You are someone who has visibility into my work and how others may experience me.

I would love to get feedback from you. I am giving you permission to be 100 percent honest with me. In fact, it's the only way I will be able to make the best course adjustments. Please don't hold back, and know that I welcome good and bad news. I am here to listen and learn.

I'd like to ask you four specific questions. You can go into as much detail as you want. In fact, the more detail you give, the more it will help me. Would that be OK with you?

What advice do you have about how to succeed here and what has worked for you?

This question has two purposes: People will open up when you are asking for advice (which is comfortable and fun) rather than feedback (which can be uncomfortable and more difficult). It will act as a way to build rapport. But if you listen closely, you will learn more about how company politics work in your organization.

How do you think others perceive me?

Do not ask "How do *you* perceive me?" because you will inevitably run up against the human aversion to conflict. When you are asking someone to look you in the eye and tell you what's wrong, it takes time to build the trust needed to get good information. But it is far easier to ask about how others may view us.

What is the one thing you think would make the biggest positive difference for my success here?

The reason this is vague is because it allows for a broad spectrum of feedback including a work skill, a personal interaction adjustment, a communication skill, or any other observation that could create an accurate picture. Leave it open for all the possibilities rather than narrowing the question, or you may miss great feedback.

What is your understanding of what I do here?
This will surprise you. People may pick up on things that were nothing more than small blips to you, and conversely, some of your most meaningful contributions may be invisible. The answer will also provide you with information about how well you are managing up and down the organization and how you need to improve your communication on key projects or deliverables.

FINAL THOUGHTS

The truth is that unless you take responsibility for understanding with clarity how you are perceived, you'll never know "it" is coming, whatever "it" is—whether a demotion, a team shift, or even getting fired. Likewise, if you are waiting and hoping you'll make the cut for a top-talent development plan, you are wasting precious time.

Be the boss of your own career by driving the feedback conversation from Day One. True to my promise to make you uncomfortable, once you get the hang of proactively seeking feedback, it's time to raise the stakes. In the chapter 7 we're going to keep getting uncomfortable by diving into the topic of conflict. You'll find that some of the best moves you can make for your career are often born from a place of disagreement—you just have to know the truth about how to harness the power of conflict.

WALKAWAY ASSIGNMENT

Now that you have a better idea of how to ask for and pay attention to feedback, make an action plan for yourself:

1. Create a list of questions you can have at the ready for quick, casual check-ins with your manager.
2. Write down your immediate and long-term areas of concern so you have them ready for the next sit-down with your manager.
3. Don't have a regular check-in time on the calendar with your manager? Ask if they would be willing to meet with you more regularly to catch up. Even a monthly or quarterly lunch or coffee meeting can get you more clarity.

5

Lies About Power

Lie: If you work hard, you'll be rewarded.

*Truth: Working hard isn't the same as
adding value. You need to do both.*

See it. Solve it. Then the company will see you. That's the essence of what playing in the gap means. But people often don't focus on that. Instead, people often gravitate to wanting more clarity around their job description.

Let's get this one thing straight: your job description is a piece of garbage. It was probably written by someone in human resources late at night so they could get the job posted first thing in the morning. Even if it was written by fancy consultants and you work for a big company, the job description can be counted on to be more general than specific and more stodgy than inspiring. A job description isn't intended to be your road map. Instead, think of it as guardrails to keep you pointed in the right direction. Your real job is to solve problems within the sphere of responsibility the job description sets out for you.

If you follow the job description perfectly, you are going
to miss the real job. You have to use some emotional
intelligence to sort out the job on paper from the job itself.

One of the most common lies that get people to this point is that if they work hard at their job as it is described, they will be rewarded accordingly. It would be nice if the equation were that simple. But getting pay increases is inextricably tied to adding value, not just working hard. It's easy to be lulled into thinking you are adding value when in fact you are just getting work done. Make no mistake, there is a difference. Author Seth Godin was absolutely correct when he said, "Not adding value is the same as taking it away."

It simply isn't true that if you focus on working hard, the rest will take care of itself. It's a good start to be a hard worker, but that alone isn't enough. Hard workers are great only when they pair that hard work with working on the right things. I've seen plenty of hard workers either never progress up the career ladder or progress very slowly. Managers do love a hard worker, and I've had people on my own team that I knew I could count on to do the work. But the idea of being a "steady worker" isn't nearly as appealing as being the person who can create momentum *and* work hard.

Steady workers are necessary, but they are
not the ones who get the big raises or promotions.

In the succession planning world, we call steady employees "solid performers." In talent management strategy, companies tag these people with a plan to give them a standard increase and let them keep working hard. But these are not the people who are tapped for accelerated promotion paths, mentoring, or training to move up in the company.

The people whose careers take off or who are tagged as top performers are those who have one strength in common: they see and solve the biggest problems holding the business back within their sphere of influence.

I've had team members whom I would categorize as superstars. They have learned how to create impact, and not just work hard. Because of it, they are ripe for promotions because I trust they can get results. The superstars have an ability to cut through all the minutiae that lands on their desk. They approach work like an emergency triage exercise: The most important lifesaving task happens first, followed by the next most important task, and so on. They call in other experts to help when needed and they are focused on fixing what is broken.

I've also had employees who work incredibly hard whom I would categorize only as a good team member. These individuals seem to do the work as it comes in without any regard to correct prioritization. They may work more hours, but their impact is not as great. Given the choice between a hard worker who sees all work as equal or a hard-enough worker who knows how to make an impact and choose the right work, I'll take hard-enough all day long.

A "hard-enough" worker who is making an impact beats a hard worker working on the wrong things.

Problem-solvers get promoted. To be seen as a problem-solver, a person must know how to get to the heart of what isn't working. It requires you to lift your head up and pull away from the daily grind to see where gaps exist. "But I did my job!" only addresses the status quo and the bare minimum of what is required. It will keep you safely in your seat—but it won't get you a seat at the table.

The people who create real impact are the ones tapped for other projects, discussed privately for new roles on the horizon, and taken care of behind closed doors. Those are the people you want to watch. They see and solve problems that hold the company back and stop leaning on an incomplete job description for guidance. They understand the concept of what I call "playing in the gap."

In this chapter, we'll dig into that concept so you can learn how to move your career forward by working smarter, not harder.

GETTING TO KNOW THE GAP

Every company is dueling between two different visions. One is the company's vision of itself—the way its people talk about what the company is striving to be; the other is the reality of what the company currently is, flaws and all.

Think of it like a house. When you are interviewing for the job, you hear about a beautiful, glistening palace. The grounds are immaculate and the pool is sparkling. It's a dream house, an architectural wonder with down-filled couches and windows two stories high in every room. The surround-sound audio system plays your favorite music as the smell of steaks sizzling on the grill wafts in from the back patio, where you and your friends will watch the sun set over a meal.

The other house—the actual house—represents how the company works today. As you get close, you realize it could use a coat of paint, and the fence needs repair. While there is a plan to get the house in top shape, inside it is still under construction. The pool might even be a blow-up pool from Walmart for now. And you're eating hot dogs and warm punch for dinner, while watching the sun set behind a new subdivision that is also still under construction.

In reality, most houses exist somewhere in between these two extremes. Houses in the "gap" have some really great features and some things that may need a bit of work to remedy. They're not quite a mansion but not quite a shack, either. Companies, their departments, and the roles in those departments are like that too. Gaps abound. What they want to be versus the realities of what they actually are is far apart. And while this isn't necessarily fatal to a company's success, the employees are the ones who get stuck trying to navigate the gaps.

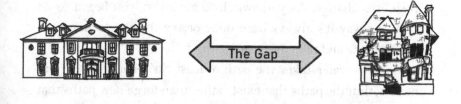

Cullyn Cowell

Every single job at every level of the company has a "gap." Customer service may have a "gap" because there is no set process on how to handle a certain common customer complaint, and there is a loss of business as a result. Recruiting may have a gap between managers and recruiters that slows down the posting of jobs or the offer process. Sales may have a gap in that existing customers aren't contacted and tracked well for upsells.

Often employees ignore these gaps and just work around them. A bad process continues, and everyone knows it's a problem, but rather than tackling it, people just keep working within the same broken world. Over time, many individuals accept it as part of the broken company for which they work.

Seeing the gaps—and your urgency around fixing them—seems to taper off the longer you are in a company. Consider when you first start a new job. There is about a six-month period where you have fresh eyes to see the company for what it is: you see flaws and strengths, great competitive advantages, and dysfunctional processes and behaviors. But as you get into the routine of your role and the "way things are," you begin to work around the problems and accept them as a part of the company dynamic. You might get acclimated to what is both good and bad in the company. As you do so, your efforts to fix what is broken may shift to learning a work-around path so you can get your job done. Your fresh eyes change. As you switch to autopilot, you begin to do work the way it's always been done or try to move around the broken parts and take the easier path.

Much as water takes the path of least resistance, it's easy to move within the paths that exist rather than forge new paths that could create better, faster flow. Playing in the gap requires you to find those "fresh eyes" again.

HOW DO I KNOW WHICH GAPS TO TACKLE?

Every department has a "vein of gold" to be discovered, but you have to get outside the constraints of your job description to find it. If you are focused on winning by doing a helluva job following your job description, I assure you that you have already begun to fall behind. You heard me right: where you *don't* go to identify gaps is your job description. I am actually advocating to move past your job description to begin the process of adding value. Stick with me on this point. So often, people make their focus the duties outlined in their flawed job description.

A disclaimer: I'm not suggesting that you should ignore your job description completely. No one gets to choose their own adventure in a company. But everyone does get to define how they will make their mark within broadly defined duties and objectives. The "gaps" are likely where you can find ways to do that. Keep the job description in context as a broad guideline and know that its purpose has never and will never be a clearly paved road along which all of your questions will be answered.

Your best bet is to look up from your job description and pay attention to what's happening around you. Look for the problems holding the company back from what it wants to be (the best, fastest, smartest) versus what it is (flawed and imperfect). The gap is what lives between these two vantage points. It's where you create change to help the company move along the continuum toward the vision company leaders have for themselves. It is where value lies for the company.

Rarely is the problem that you can't find a gap at all to work on. Rather, the challenge is deciding which one to tackle first.

Go where the low-hanging fruit is.
Pick the gaps where you can win.

Don't fall on your sword by picking the gap with the highest degree of difficulty. If you've ever heard Dave Ramsey talk about debt consolidation, his advice is to work the small debts first, then move to the big ones like your mortgage. My advice is the same. Your goal is to build a track record of solving problem after problem. Go for the small wins. Build from there. But don't start with the one problem that's so complex you have only 50/50 odds of getting it solved.

Take some time to identify the "right" gaps.

GAP CASE STUDIES

To help you see how gaps are found at every stage of your career, let's look at some real-world examples, starting with my own experience in identifying and filling a gap.

CASE STUDY: EARLY-CAREER GAP

I was working early in my career as a recruiter at Covey Leadership Center, Stephen R. Covey's company where the 7 *Habits* book and courses were born. My job was to search the world for presenters who could teach *The 7 Habits of Highly Effective People* at the pinnacle of Covey's success. This was more than a full-time job, given that we were selling the course to companies much faster than we could deliver. In the course of identifying and interviewing candidates, I accidentally stumbled into an affirmative action–compliance requirement our human resources department knew nothing about. This was a government-mandated program intended to increase diversity in companies. To give a bit of context, the company was in Utah, where it was very white, and very male-dominated.

As I studied, I realized that this compliance requirement was important for more than one reason: We were an international company with a stellar reputation. We had been lucky enough to fly under the radar without realizing we needed to put a plan in place.

This was something that, in my view as recruiter, was a problem for the company that needed to be solved.

Deciding to take it on with the blessing of my manager, I quickly realized this was not sexy work. It was hard and analytical and didn't play to my strengths. Several months into this side project, we received notification that we were being randomly audited on our plan. With only a basic knowledge of what this was, affirmative action suddenly took front and center for our young company. As the "expert" (of three months), I was suddenly an important person to the company. We developed the plan at warp speed and rallied the management team around the requirements. Fast-forwarding to the end of the audit, we passed with flying colors.

That one project did more to accelerate my career than anything I have done since. I found the gap that never would have shown up on my job description, and hands down started solving the problem. I was labeled as the go-to person even though I was in an early career job.

CASE STUDY: MID-CAREER GAP

Josh was hired as the head of recruiting to fill a difficult niche of door-to-door salespeople. This was a difficult hire because the position was 100 percent commission, and it required discipline and nerves of steel to be rejected day after day, knocking on door after door to persuade homeowners to let complete strangers into their home for a sales presentation. To make it even more difficult, the salespeople were used to recruiting their own sales teams and did not have confidence that anyone else could sell the opportunity like they could.

As you can imagine, the turnover in a direct sales group is high under the best of circumstances—and this wasn't the best of circumstances. Team leaders were under pressure to increase the number of salespeople by more than 25 percent overnight. And the approach to hire friends and friends of friends could only take the sales leaders so far.

Josh did not come from a recruiting background and was hired in part for his social media savvy and his experience in helping B-list actors and "has-beens" find popularity again through social media and viral video campaigns. The very idea that Josh had no relevant recruiting experience but understood how to use social media and digital marketing skills was exactly why he was hired for the job that sales didn't want him in to begin with.

Josh quickly grasped that the real problem was that nobody in sales wanted a recruiter. The leaders wanted to recruit on their own, in part because they were excellent at selling the candidate on the opportunity and felt they had better odds of getting the candidate over the finish line. But they were doing it one discussion at a time. Rather than fighting a battle he could not win, Josh instead pivoted away from being a recruiter selling the opportunity toward being a marketing funnel to attract talent. He set up a social media campaign to attract the right personalities to the company and filtered them into glitzy sales recruiting events where the leaders just had to show up and make the right pitch to a ready-made audience of candidates.

Instead of the leaders finding and recruiting their own talent individually, Josh found dozens of candidates at a time and created the right environment for sales leaders to do what they do best: sell the role! He knew about branding, so he branded the hell out of these events, producing crazy ideas like scavenger hunts, giant Jenga tournaments, and race car–driving events or bringing in famous athletes or social media influencers to speak.

Josh knew that the gap was in finding candidates and quickly handing them over. He also knew if we were to achieve the right volume targets for hiring, sales leaders did not have the time or the skill set to orchestrate a grand recruiting event that would be supportive of the vision they wanted to paint for the candidate. Branding the events to attract the typical mid-twenties applicant required a special touch.

Josh and his team of $15-an-hour "creatives" were able to increase the pipeline far beyond 25 percent and earn a callout from an analyst on one of the company's quarterly public reports who wondered out loud what the magic formula was for the company's recruiting traction. While there were many people responsible for all the pieces that made this effort work, Josh understood his gap. Had he come in and behaved like a traditional recruiter, he would have quit in frustration early into the job. Instead, he stopped paying attention to his job title of recruiter, quickly reassessed the company dynamics, and shifted from recruiter to marketing and lead magnet specialist. He filled the gap beautifully.

CASE STUDY: SENIOR CAREER

Sarshar was the senior leader over all operations. Although he wasn't new in this role, a company reorganization had placed a new department—CAD design—under his care. He quickly realized there were some problems that needed to be fixed. As he began to look at the performance metrics, he realized how different the output was from person to person for rooftop solar design proposals. Some people were fast, and some were slow. Some delivered a correct design, while others made multiple mistakes and rework had to be done. Part of the problem was the variation of the work, but the other part was the incredibly high turnover rates for the team. These were $15/hour employees who would leave to make another dollar an hour at any company that offered it up.

Sarshar realized that even though his job was to create operational efficiencies, the real problem was high turnover and the inability to keep any institutional knowledge in the department. As soon as someone was trained and up to speed, they left. Where a traditional leader may have increased the pay for the whole team and busted the budget, Sarshar saw the opportunity to play in the gap.

He pitched an innovative new pay plan that would play to the temperament of the millennials. While new team members would start at the same rate of pay, every single month the pay would move up or down for each individual based upon how many accurate CAD designs they could finish. His modeling and assumptions showed he could give raises of as much as 50 percent to top performers and it would not increase the company costs because the increase in pay was tied to an uplift in the number of CAD designs a person could produce. On the other end of the spectrum, those who could not produce the work would make much less. Every single month was a new starting point for the individual to try again.

The immediate alignment between pay and performance and the gamification of the department drove increased levels of CAD production because individuals could see the direct correlation between their quality of work and their pay. The increase in pay also kept them at the company long enough to see other career paths they could move into and continue to grow. Turnover changed dramatically, and the company began to lose only those who did not have the aptitude for the role. The changes paid for themselves!

Sarshar realized his role wasn't to simply push the team harder or hire more people to solve the turnover problem. He saw the true gap.

For all these individuals, playing in the gap created success they would not have had otherwise. It created alternatives that opened even more possibilities:

- For me, playing in the gap helped me be seen as the go-to person, and I was given more responsibilities and promotions.
- For Josh, it made him the hero in an organization that was ready to completely reject his presence; he showed how he could complement the sales leaders' skills with his own to create a solution nobody had ever defined in a job description.
- For Sarshar, he created a path for top performers to stay without creating any additional costs to the company.

PICKING THE RIGHT GAPS

You can actually use the acronym GAP to lead your thought process when it comes to choosing the right areas to focus on: First, think about whether the gap will help you take your role or team from good to great. Next, consider your access to the issue at hand. Finally, consider what your plan might be to solve the problem.

- **G: Good to Great:** "Can solving this help move my function/role/department from good to great? Are the impacts meaningful? Does it help things move faster and/or be more efficient? What outcomes would show meaningful movement?"
- **A: Access:** "Can this problem get fixed with action I could take? Do I have the skills, tools, autonomy, and knowledge to have a clear vision on how to solve this?"
- **P: Plan:** "What are the first steps I need to take? What three next steps will create traction? Am I clear on how I'll know each step is complete?"

GAP WORKSHEET

As you move through the Gap Worksheet on the following page, think about these tips to help you find additional clarity:

- The first rule of picking the right gap is to pick the one where you can win.
- Start looking at simple gaps you can control fully within your role.
- If you want to win bigger, close a critical gap that helps the whole department and requires collaboration with others in your department.
- If you can close a critical gap that links to the company initiatives, you can win big; it doesn't have to be hard or

GAP WORKSHEET

	CONSIDERATIONS	THE PROBLEM AND THE PLAN
⟷ **GAP**	What isn't working right? What slows business or processes down? What is being overlooked that could give better business results? Is there an action or outcome I can control that aligns to company initiatives?	
EVIDENCE	What data or evidence do I have that tells me there is a problem?	
DESIRED OUTCOMES	How would I know I've solved this problem? What would success look like? If you can, detail how you would measure improvement.	

	CONSIDERATIONS	THE PROBLEM AND THE PLAN
ACCESS	What do I need in order to take this on? People/Teams Tools Budget Skills Buy-in	

	CONSIDERATIONS	THE PROBLEM AND THE PLAN
PLAN	What is the first step I can take to solve it? 01. 02.	

Ahmed Khalid Khan

complex to be strategic to the company—it just has to be selected well.

- If you select a gap that feels strategic and fraught with risk, slow down and reassess.
- You don't have to map the entire solution at once; being three steps ahead is good enough.

If you are hesitant about selecting a gap because you don't think your role can make a difference, start small to give yourself confidence. My observations convince me that it doesn't matter if you are the entry-level front desk person or the vice president of operations. Every single level has opportunities to make a significant difference within its sphere.

You might think that you have to be at least at mid-level with the right title or department to fill a gap that anyone cares about. But this simply isn't true. Anyone can solve problems, and there is a different set of pros and cons depending on what level of role you hold within a company.

Solving Gaps in Junior Roles

Upside: Starting at a junior level, you get to pick challenges that are less complex. This is great news because you can produce a solution to a problem and start fixing it without a lot of fanfare, approvals, or red tape. See it. Solve it. And oftentimes, you don't have to implement the solution by yourself. You can find what's wrong, test a solution, show that it works, and then get the support of a leader to help roll out a solution more broadly to the team. You can get lots of little wins and be known as a problem-solver very quickly. You have the benefit of volume on your side. You can even afford to have a few that aren't smashing successes.

Downside: For the people who are ready to move up from a junior role, complexity will slow them down in the volume department. They need to choose their gaps more wisely and follow them through to the end with a lot of eyeballs watching them.

Solving Gaps in Mid to Senior Roles

Upside: The higher you go in a company, the greater reach you typically have. Often you have more influence and opportunities for collaboration across departments. If you are on a manager track, you have more budget and more resources you can put into a project without needing the support of others. Another advantage is you often have access to people who can do the reporting or analysis on metrics that change drives.

Downside: The higher you go, the more complex the problems. They cannot be solved by you alone. And when you don't have all the control for the outcome, there is an element of risk.

SAMPLE GAPS

I want to open your eyes to the many types of contributions that can be made throughout an organization. All of these are real solutions from people over the course of my career, many of whom were junior-level employees:

- **The information gap:** An assistant put all the past and present board meeting materials into a central online repository, eliminating lost or misplaced materials as well as costly printing and shipping charges.

- **The speed gap:** A developer built an onboarding app to get sales employees hired in thirty minutes and managers notified as each step was completed, decreasing job-offer-to-start-date times by five days and increasing first-week productivity by 50 percent.
- **The perks gap:** An employee had the idea to replace the company kitchen and its contracted chefs with local vendors who delivered lunch orders for the company, saving $2 million a year.
- **The education gap:** A finance team put together a basic P&L training for all employees to help make everyone act more like an owner and understand the company budgets as well as the results that were shared in quarterly meetings.
- **The customer gap:** A supervisor developed a comp structure where hourly pay would move up or down each month based on three key quality and volume metrics. This allowed for top performers to always be paid the most and all but eliminated unwanted turnover.
- **The candidate gap:** A recruiting manager who had no more budget to hire but needed to increase candidate flow by 25 percent rolled out a campaign to make every employee a recruiter, giving tickets for each referral into a drawing for an all-expenses-paid trip to Hawaii. The solution was funded by external recruiting cost savings.
- **The contract gap:** A senior employee who could see that many of our contracts needed to be renegotiated suggested that he could take over the process and get a percentage of the savings he created. He ended up

making more than $200,000 in a year but saved the company well over $2 million.

- **The innovations gap:** An admin who helped put together quarterly state-of-the-company meetings saw that by telling the right stories, we could create a culture of innovation. He started an innovation program (funded by the CEO's office) that shared in a $5,000 prize for the best employee ideas to improve the company.
- **The "what we didn't know" gap:** An employee who filled in dozens of applications for government rebates each day decided to research the program and found the company could eliminate portions of the manual entry, allowing the company to process 50 percent more forms per day and bringing in millions in additional revenue.

FINAL THOUGHTS

I've found that clients who play in the gap are more likely to pitch new experimental roles in their companies, they are better at focusing on measuring their outcomes (because they have to be clear on what they are trying to accomplish from the outset), and they are more likely to be noticed in their organizations.

It's worth mentioning you still need to focus on elements of your job that need to be done, and some of those are focused not on solving problems, but on "keeping the wheels on." But rather than spending 80 percent of your time maintaining and only 20 percent playing in the gap, a worthy goal is to create more efficient ways to streamline the maintenance work. If you do this, you can shift the percentage so that a greater amount of your time is spent focusing on solving problems that are holding the company back. The more time you spend on solving problems instead of maintaining, the more promotable you become.

I hope you'll never see your job description the same way again.

WALKAWAY ASSIGNMENT

It's time to find your own gaps. Think about the career stage you are currently in. What gaps can you identify? Make a short list. Then, brainstorm ways you can fill the gaps. Are you in a mid- or senior-stage career? Look back at your time as a new employee and do some hindsight thinking to identify gaps that you were too nervous to fill at that time.

Would you do anything differently if you knew then what you know now?

6

Lies About the
Corner Office

Lie: The ones with the budget and title have all the power.

Truth: Knowledge is power.

One of the most powerful people I knew wasn't a CEO. He wasn't even an executive. He was a mid-level individual contributor who sat in a cubicle and, at the time, didn't make more than $50,000. At first, he was just the quiet guy in the corner, but eventually I began to see him in different departments, eating lunch with others from all over the company. I watched his progression and noticed how his own span of influence grew.

One day I was walking past an executive's office, and there he was, alongside several other senior people. I could see he was presenting something. I could not make sense of how Cubicle Guy got in the meeting or why he was presenting. I thought at first that he was one of those corporate spies who comes in to see how the company is actually doing, but that wasn't the case. After a few years, he was tapped to be on a team that the CEO put together to research competitors, new ideas, and potential merger-and-acquisition targets. Eventually, he became the one creating the slide decks for investors and following up with other executives on critical projects the CEO was sponsoring.

In three years, he had more than doubled his pay, and he had become an indisputable person of influence in the organization. Cubicle Guy had no Harvard education. He was neither the CEO's nephew nor a rich trust fund kid whose parents got him the job. This was someone who understood that what he had to offer was seeing and solving problems in the company. His fearless approach to learning about the company gave him insights that many of our own executives didn't have. He knew the problems at the bottom, the top, and the middle. This was a person who went from nobody knowing his name to being of immense influence and power in the organization. How did he do it? He understood this principle:

If you want to gain influence in your company, become the expert of your industry, your competitors, and your company. It doesn't require an advanced degree. It requires only your curiosity.

What Cubicle Guy understood is that he could increase his influence in the organization by listening, asking questions, and acquiring new knowledge that could then be distilled into meaningful action or ideas.

People with power are people who are listened to. Their opinion is sought after, and they offer informed perspectives. I hear the belief all the time that the only people who have power are those

who have titles, corner offices, or the biggest staffs or budgets—
that if you aren't a senior leader, people won't listen to you. It
usually takes the form of one of these statements:

- *"But if I have the title, others here will treat me differently."*
- *"My manager won't let me be strategic."*
- *"I don't have the power to really make a difference at this level."*
- *"Other people are making the real decisions and I just have to do what I'm told."*

Stop it.

There are plenty of people who didn't have the right title or the
corner office but who have influenced the course of events where
they work. Companies need people of influence at all levels. Any
person at any level has access to making a difference. If senior
leadership is where you believe all the power lies, then you are
wasting the opportunity right in front of you to use your role,
right now, to begin becoming a person of power.

Cubicle Guy, an everyday individual, helped the leadership
team see a gap in the competitive landscape by asking a few questions that started with "I'm curious . . ." And while he wasn't the
originator of the company strategy, he was able to create a compelling story and presentation for road shows to raise new inves-
tor money.

He developed an innovation contest where the best ideas were
funded, and employees could win a percentage of the cost savings
or revenue brought in. This opened up the idea that every employee
could make a difference. It resulted in millions of dollars through
new products, new revenue streams, and great cost-saving ideas.

While it would be difficult to tie back to Cubicle Guy every dollar he saved or made for the company, his influence was felt throughout the organization.

The power of one person can be enormous. Even a person buried deep in an organization.

In this chapter, I'll show you the formula for building influence and teach you how becoming a curator of knowledge can make you more valuable to the company. I will also help you learn how to translate your results into data that you can share with leadership to get support for your ideas. You'll begin to see how to use knowledge and data to expand your voice in the organization.

THE FORMULA FOR INFLUENCE

Part of the mindset change that's required to grow your influence is learning to have a voice.

You may think that you have nothing valuable to say, but the more you seek out information and knowledge, the more confident you'll feel. To have influence, at a bare minimum you need to have a point of view; otherwise you'll be a "ghost" in your organization. You have to be seen and heard to create influence. Not in a reckless kind of way, but in an intentional way where you share what you know and are not fearful that you aren't "senior enough," "smart enough," or "knowledgeable enough." This can be anxiety-inducing to those in an early-stage career. But remember, having a voice also has a secondary benefit of increasing your satisfaction.

You won't have influence until you stop believing it's everyone else's job to figure everything out.

The second key principle of creating influence is to get curious! When you begin to ask questions, you will not only understand the company better, but you'll also begin to see outside of your department and into the entire ecosystem! Suddenly, how departments fit together will make more sense. You'll be better informed on how strategy translates down through the organization, and you'll be more attuned to why your role is important and how you can make a difference. Curiosity can help you pick the right gap projects or open up career paths you might not have known existed. It's a bit like knowing exactly how the computer operates and not just what it spits out.

When you intersect what you are learning about the company and the industry with what you already know about your own areas of interest and expertise, you may be surprised by how much knowledge you have.

As simple as it sounds, there are three key "Stops" and three "Starts" that begin the process of gaining power in a company.

STOP

- Stop waiting for someone else to define the problems or give the answers.
- Stop waiting on permission to fix them.
- Stop feeling you don't have the right to have an opinion.

START

- Start asking questions—get curious.
- Start connecting the dots on the data.
- Start speaking up and asking, "What if . . . ?"

To illustrate this, let me show you what an entry-level recruiter was able to contribute by daring to have a voice. As a Stage 1 employee, she was able to apply her specialized knowledge to a company challenge in an incredibly meaningful way.

CASE STUDY: RECRUITING WHEN THE MONEY RAN OUT

The heads turned all at once like a movie in slow motion. The junior recruiter, the quietest one on the team, had just offered up an idea that caused everyone to do a double take.

We were in a staffing meeting discussing the customer service roles we couldn't fill. There were too many employers competing for talent in the college community, and our team was falling behind. The needs of the company were impossible parameters. No new budget money. The budget we had was the budget we got. And yet we had to increase the number of applicants and hires we brought in. The manager of the department wanted to know if anyone had any ideas, no matter how crazy they were. The room was quiet, filled with discouragement. They had already tried everything they knew. Amid grumblings and a few ideas such as doing more career fairs or changing up the job posting, the recruiter spoke up and voiced this disruptive idea:

"What if we made every employee a recruiter?" she asked.

The comment sat in the air for a moment, and then all the heads nodded in agreement, amazed at the simplicity of her statement. She continued, "If we don't have money, let's meet the college students where they're at—their social media accounts." Her comment started a robust discussion that ended in a brilliant and crazy plan that actually worked.

With the input of the rest of the team, they rolled out a program where every employee participated by posting on social media their own creative video about why they loved working at the company. The recruiting team provided social media filters and a link that employees could use to get people to apply from their individual profiles. Each week the most viral post got a ticket for a drawing for a trip for two to Hawaii (paid for by eliminating one budgeted search fee during the year). For every applicant who applied and named an employee as their referral, another ticket was given. And employees whose referrals were hired received two tickets.

The program was a wild success. The positions were filled, and the recruiting team saved the day. All because one person applied their knowledge of social media and the college mindset to the problem. That's the secret sauce in the formula for gaining influence.

The idea in itself was incredibly powerful, but the real power came in the data that backs up the success of the program. The team increased referrals by 40 percent over four months and increased applicants from 228 to 425 per month. Ultimately, it *reduced* (rather than increased) the cost to hire by 25 percent and gave a whole new channel to continue driving the department efficiency. The application of your specialized knowledge is the sundae, and the data is the cherry on top.

USING DATA AS POWER

Data is limitless! It's available everywhere you look in a company. Even if you don't have data, you can create it by measuring the work you do. It may sound like a big idea to think that you could find valuable data that others aren't using yet and move the needle on the business, but it's true! A massive amount of unstructured data exists in companies, meaning it isn't formulated into any particular report. This is called "dark data," and most estimates say that 80 to 90 percent of the data a company holds is in this category.

As an executive, I can tell you that it's already a challenge to consume the 10 to 20 percent of the data that is structured and cull from it the points that help us make better business decisions. But we are leaving vast amounts of information untouched, which tells you companies don't have a perfect view of the data and may not even be seeing important parts at all!

Companies are never finished discovering the data that helps shape them, which is why you can use your data and your unique perspective. It may be the difference maker. There are always new data "finds" that everyday people in everyday roles discover. It is a bit like going to Crater of Diamonds State Park in Arkansas. It's one of the only places in the world where people can search for diamonds in their original volcanic source and keep what they find. More than six hundred diamonds are found each year. People have hunted diamonds there since 1906, and yet every year there are new diamonds found, as evidenced by a 4.38 yellow diamond found in 2021.

You can find a data diamond in your company as well.

I'm not exaggerating when I call data a diamond. McKinsey recently published findings that companies with the greatest overall growth in revenue and earnings are attributing their data and analytics initiatives to at least 20 percent of their earnings over the past three years. These organizations are starting to make data part of the mindset from the frontline worker to the CEO, realizing it is part of their formula for success. Is it that farfetched to think you could have similar results in your own role if you begin to treat data as your competitive advantage?

The previous chapter addressed the idea that you can increase your power by playing in the gap. Can you imagine if you could get a similar 20 percent lift on the outcomes of your gap projects by using knowledge and data in more deliberate ways?

CASE STUDY: I MAY HAVE FOUND SOMETHING . . .

At one of the biggest established fintech companies in the nation, it was a mid-level product manager, and not an executive, who discovered how clients could use a new product offering to get a massive uplift in volume. It's important to note this new product was already developed and already being sold before this data diamond was ever discovered! The manager was looking at the transaction data stream of the company's top twenty customers when he found some patterns that piqued his interest. He ran the numbers again, this time over a five-year horizon, and realized the markers of the customer buying patterns suggested this newer product could potentially increase the customers' transaction volumes by about 50 percent. This was never identified in the original product plans or any of the ROI modeling that had been done.

He walked into his manager's office and said, "I think I may have found something."

They quickly put together a test group of top customers; the first customer came back with a pretty extraordinary "something": adopting this product had uplifted their transaction volumes by 73 percent.

This is unheard of, especially in a company of this size and maturity. Yet a curious product manager with a penchant for data diving landed on a disruptive change that gave the company's revenue stream a lift. This data diamond was found because someone understood the power of data.

I've used early stage examples for a reason. If you are comfortable with using data from out of the gate, it will become second nature later in your career. It is the language of business and especially of senior leaders. Which brings me to this point:

If you put off learning that language, you are missing an opportunity to be truly heard by the senior leaders of the organization.

TEN PRACTICAL WAYS TO USE DATA

Individuals in companies often feel they have more to offer than their leaders understand. The fastest way to fix this isn't screaming and jumping up and down. It's not by threatening to leave the company. There's a simple fix. If you want your leader to see you, talk the language of numbers. If you are unsure where to start or how you can use data to increase your personal power, here are a few ideas from Bryan Christiansen, one of the most gifted operations executives I know. He is a lifelong learner on the study of productivity and has a knack for making difficult concepts feel accessible to all levels:

- **Negotiating a raise:** Bring data to the table such as the tangible value you add; remember that the business hires you to achieve results; don't ask for a raise based on emotional arguments such as, "I feel like I am underpaid."

- **Working on that next promotion:** Bring data to the table that outlines that you are ready for that big promotion; align data with what your boss wants to accomplish. Data such as certificates or trainings completed that show you have the required skills is more helpful than emotional arguments such as, "I have been here the longest and deserve the promotion."
- **Leading a team:** Share a vision that is backed by data; give your team a tangible "reason to believe." Teams want to win just as individuals want to win.
- **Pitching a new proposal:** Understand what the approval criteria will be and bring data that shows the proposal meets and exceeds all criteria; remember that approval criteria is tied with the decision maker and their view of what a win looks like.
- **Selling a solution to a client:** Understand what winning looks like for the client and customize the presentation to their goals; bring data that shows your solution will help them achieve their goals.
- **Giving and receiving feedback:** Focus on sharing real data versus unsubstantiated broad statements; ask for data to help you better understand feedback received; remember that feedback situations can be emotional.
- **Negotiating with vendors:** Understand what winning looks like for them, then balance it with what winning looks like for you and your company; bring data to drive your points home.
- **Interacting with customers as a customer advocate:** Understand that everyone wants to be heard; when customers are upset and emotional, sharing data may be your only route to resolving their concern.

- **Identifying why a business process has broken down:** Bring data; remember that people who are part of the process are not machines and have feelings.
- **Crafting marketing talking points:** Customers are looking to achieve something when making a purchase; identify their goals; understand what your company brings to the table to address their needs; gather market research; bring data that supports your conclusions.

In addition to knowing how to use data, you should also learn the key metrics for your department and how they matter to the company. When you know the data that drives your department or industry, you can use it to make positive changes for your role or within your department, no matter your starting point.

Every role has metrics. They may not even be defined yet, but if they aren't, don't wait on someone else. Determine the best metrics to show progression in the work you do. This is a natural way for you to focus on work the company cares about. There's a secondary benefit of measuring your work: it can result in powerful bullet points you can use as leverage to ask for more responsibility (because you have shown you understand how to help the company with Job #1), or more money, or eventually to show on your next resume for a maximum offer.

Here is a list of potential metrics you can consider as you build your own personal or department scorecard:

METRICS TO CONSIDER

- Percentage increased
- Budget managed

- Money saved
- Revenue generated
- Sales increased
- Profits increased
- Number of processes improved or steps in process reduced
- Customer loyalty scores increased
- Web traffic (or people visiting your app or system) increased
- Order fulfillment time decreased
- Employee or customer engagement increased
- Lead conversion rates increased
- Order fulfillment numbers or speed increased
- Increased percentage of repeat customers

BEING A CURATOR OF KNOWLEDGE

If you read the best practices from influential CEOs, many cite that a regular part of their day includes reading up on current events and business news. It needs to be part of your daily practice as well.

You can extract incredible value from all the knowledge you gather, both in and outside the company. Reading and learning about new trends, innovation, and technology always pays dividends. Even if it has nothing to do with your exact job, it may trigger an idea that could change how you do work, or even how your company sees itself.

To begin, start by becoming a student of your role or area of expertise. Then gather information from outside sources about your industry, the competitors, and emerging trends. Lastly, expand into your own company.

Here are five practical ways you can gather information:

1. **Current news:** Spent fifteen minutes a day reading business news or respected business publications. Look for emerging trends, ideas, and new companies or products relevant to your company or practice area.

2. **Department dashboards:** Ask your manager if there are any dashboards or metrics tracked for the department. Dig into them and see if you can identify any weaknesses, strengths, gaps, or opportunities.

3. **Professional affiliations:** Join relevant industry or professional associations. Consider national organizations with local chapters where you have frequent events to hear speakers, network, and learn about emerging trends.

4. **Company quarterly results:** If you are a publicly traded company, listen to the quarterly results and guidance from your company. You will hear some great nuggets about company direction and challenges that might not make it to your own department.

5. **Local top business awards:** These are often sponsored by a local business group or magazine. You will be exposed to best practices, new ideas, and individuals who have created impact in your local business scene.

The wonderful thing about knowledge is that it's additive. Knowing more about the company, your department, or the industry in which you work cannot take you backward. When you add new knowledge to what you already know, it can do only one thing: reinforce the direction you are already going or give information to make an adjustment.

SOURCES FOR NEWS AND BUSINESS CURRENT EVENTS

- *Wall Street Journal*: One of the strongest publications for current business, investing, and financial news.
- *Forbes*: Comprehensive content covering stock market, finance, innovation, M&A, technology, and careers. Popular lists including "World's Most Valuable Brands" and "The World's Billionaires."
- *Fortune*: Best known for its Fortune 500 list, which ranks businesses by revenue. It also features annual lists of the "100 Best Companies to Work For" and "Most Powerful Women."
- *Harvard Business Review*: Some refer to this as the executive bible, with well-researched articles on current business trends, especially within tech innovation. A C-suite favorite.
- *Fast Company*: Millennial look and feel that tends to focus on innovative ideas and changes in the business world.
- **MarketWatch:** The site is known particularly for its continuous coverage of stock market updates.
- *Inc.*: Good for entrepreneurs and start-ups, with thousands of articles on starting and growing a business, angel financing, sales and marketing, innovation, and more.

- **Clubhouse app:** Originally founded by California venture capitalists as a platform to discuss upcoming companies and industry trends. Now it has extended to many other topics but still leans heavily toward innovative trends and start-ups.

This formula will not lead you astray. In fact, let's move to the end of the story about Cubicle Guy. He's not sitting in a cubicle anymore. He's a marketing executive. As he should be.

Whether being an executive or simply an individual contributor recognized fully for all you can contribute, it is within your grasp. You don't need permission. All that's required is right in front of you.

FINAL THOUGHTS

Power is not always about your title. More often than not, power is about your influence. Anyone at a company can have influence—you just need to know how to use your knowledge to get it. Think about some of the most invaluable people in your office, from the mailroom to the C-suite. People who are widely trusted within an organization are those who not only hold knowledge but know how to use it to drive results within their sphere of influence.

Don't fall for the lie that power only resides in the C-suite. You can use your unique knowledge set to grow your influence laterally so that you become one of the most trusted people in the office.

WALKAWAY ASSIGNMENT

One great way to visualize your sphere of influence and knowledge is to draw a mind map. Think about a core piece of knowledge you have that is unique to you in your company. Write it down and draw a circle around it. Then, start drawing branches out from that circle with circles on the ends of those branches. Fill those circles with all the ways you can use that knowledge at work and/or specific ways that knowledge can benefit your department. From those circles, draw more branches and circles. In those circles, write how that knowledge benefits other departments and/or the company at large. When you finish, you will have a visual representation of how far that one kernel of knowledge can reach.

7

Getting Comfortable with Conflict

Lie: I will be viewed more positively if I am easy to get along with and avoid conflict.

Truth: You won't grow in your career if you can't get comfortable with conflict.

I didn't realize I had a big mouth until the day I yelled at our chief legal counsel. I was brand-new in my first career job as an administrative assistant to the president of the acclaimed Stephen R. Covey Leadership Center. As a dewy-faced young woman, completely unprepared for the business world, I was barely figuring out how to do my job, and in the first big interaction with an executive, I had just created some very visible conflict.

On this day, our head attorney came into my office to pick up a packet the president had left for him and casually started the conversation with, "Sweetheart, would you——." Before he had a chance to even finish the sentence, my spunky self blurted out, "DON'T YOU CALL ME 'SWEETHEART'!" I use caps because I could not have been more forceful. It had no sooner come out of my mouth than I realized I had just called out a senior executive. Loudly. Where others could hear.

Talk about a way to bring conflict into your life. The words jumped out of my mouth before my brain even knew I was thinking them. But after a shocked, several-second silence where we were both mentally jockeying for first place in the awkward department, he looked at me earnestly and said, "I'm sorry. I didn't mean to do that. It won't happen again." It never did happen again, and we worked closely together the rest of my tenure.

In the moments right after I blurted it out, I thought it surely would end my career. To be fair, there are others out there who can share a similar story that did not end as well. But in my case, the conflict created a boundary that served us both. I never forgot the experience. It gave me my first taste of conflict—the fear of having it as well as its benefit of creating boundaries and stronger partnerships.

> *We avoid sharing hard information because*
> *we think it breaks trust, when it is the*
> *very thing that may be needed to build it.*

Conflict is unavoidable in the workforce. It starts in the very beginning stages of a job with an offer and a pay negotiation. If you avoid conflict or discomfort in the negotiation, the lack of conflict is already hurting you. The same is true as you continue your career. Potential conflict is everywhere, from establishing boundaries with your manager or a coworker, to fighting for your project to be funded, to disagreeing on the prioritization of a department initiative.

Every project, budget, manager-employee relationship, interdepartmental collaboration, and coworker relationship has a degree of conflict built in. Depending on which study you look at, about 80 percent of employees indicate they have recently had some form of workplace conflict. But of those who have had conflict with a manager, about one in five, or 20 percent, end up leaving the company. Another 20 percent choose never to say anything and let the resentment continue to simmer. What a shame that so much conflict goes unresolved. Especially when we know that speaking up is one of the primary drivers to create a better work experience!

Clients I work with seem to understand inherently that they need to be better at communicating in times of conflict, but they are also fearful that the conflict will break something—the relationship with the other person, their promotion path, or how they are viewed in the organization. What goes undiscussed is pay or career paths, work overload or teamwork imbalance, which demotivates those stuck with the bigger load to carry.

If you feel that you are breaking trust when you are clear and honest in difficult conversations, I argue that just the opposite is true. When I know you are telling me the truth is when I begin to trust you the most, especially when I know the opinion or feedback you are giving me isn't easy to give.

Disagreement does not have to equate to you being less likable.

Disagreement does not need to erode trust.

Disagreement alone does not damage your career.

Disagreement does not make you a difficult employee.

Individuals who can have crucial (and, yes, uncomfortable) conversations are much more likely to become trusted advisors within the organization. Those who dare to strive for a different kind of relationship with a manager—one where they share their opinions and ideas—will find they are much more likely to receive promotions. A 2019 study showed that 84 percent of employees who were engaged in active communication were recognized for their work, while only 25 percent of the less communicative employee population was recognized with positive comments or promotions.[1] If strong communication—especially the ability to have difficult conversations—can get you promoted, then the lack of these skills can have the opposite effect.

*If you can't resolve conflict,
it will function as a fatal flaw in your career.*

Getting comfortable with conflict is an essential skill set if you expect to continue growing in your career. You can walk around trying to please everyone and never confronting difficult topics with your manager or coworkers. But you will not make it to a director position if that is how you operate. There will come a point when you need to lobby for resources, fight for prioritization, or disagree with another leader. For that matter, you will have to get uncomfortable even to negotiate your pay throughout your career.

On the converse side, you can over-rotate and become a lightning rod of conflict. Don't make the mistake of thinking you must be too direct or bold to be seen. Both ends of the spectrum will hurt a career.

With such high stakes, you'll need to learn the difference between positive and negative conflict. Not understanding the difference could torpedo your efforts. You'll also need to learn a communication model to use in a potentially difficult conversation.

*Many people make the mistake of having
the right conversation the wrong way.*

THE GROUND RULES FOR CANDID CONVERSATIONS

As with all areas in your career, the way you speak involves a bit of art and a bit of science. Your words matter. How they land matters. There is middle ground between the extremes of not saying enough and saying too much. Stephen R. Covey taught me a wonderful principle early in my career that has stuck with me for more than twenty years: To build relationships, you have to balance courage *and* consideration.

It's easy to talk about a bad manager or coworker on a private Slack channel with your closest peers. It doesn't take any courage to talk about those not present. Real courage is about having a difficult conversation eyeball-to-eyeball with a person. Now that I can respect.

Here is the lie you need to understand:

*Lie: At work, if I mention a topic that is negative or
charged, it will break trust between us. If it's my manager
or someone higher up than me, my job is at risk.*

*Truth: You can talk about just about any topic when
you lead with assuming good intent in the other person.
A conversation that starts with giving one the benefit of the
doubt will almost always build, rather than break, trust.
Especially with your manager.*

If you can be honest without being reckless, you can build trust. Having the right conversation, the right way, at the right time is critically important, especially for those of you who are not managers, because an extra element of risk exists for those in a superior/subordinate power dynamic.

STRIVE FOR GOOD CONFLICT

Conflict at its core is not bad. It doesn't necessarily mean the company has a problem or that you are working in the wrong place. It is simply a sign that you are out of alignment with another person. Instead of viewing it as negative, think about it as an uncomfortable but effective way to get aligned again. Conflict has the capacity to move projects, departments, key decisions, or work relationships forward. If you view conflict as a win-lose engagement, you'll miss viewing each conflict as a conversation between trusted partners working together to find a common resolution.

Good conflict happens when two or more people are acting as partners to solve a problem. You are on the right track if your language with the other person assumes good intent.

It's easy to get stuck in thinking conflict has to be adversarial: where there is a winner and a loser. If you think conflict is about who comes out ahead in the fight, or that mastering conflict happens when you learn to "speak your mind" or "tell it like it is," you have leaned into bad conflict. This approach will not build trust. Bad conflict implies that I'm on one side and you are on the other. It's easy to see how this approach also carries with it a lot of emotion, which will only fuel the fire and take the conflict down a negative path. If you are someone who feels that conflict will require you to get louder to get your point across or that you'll need to leave damaged work relationships in your wake in order to drive your priorities forward, you've over-rotated. This does not get you ahead. You may be able to muscle a decision your way and think that's progress, but you are mistaken. It is not conflict that builds a career.

The words you use and the tone you set play a critical role in creating a safe conversation. I have found that being successful with your communication requires you to hit difficult topics head-on in a way that doesn't shut down the other party and leaves room for differing opinions. You can be a truth-teller and get to the core of an issue without using a scorched-earth approach. But you'll need to check your language because the words that individuals often use in a high-stakes conversation are filled with implied judgments that assume bad intent in the other party.

> *Those individuals who are penalized for "honest"*
> *conversations in the workplace are often people*
> *who fail to create mutual purpose and safety*
> *when they begin the conversation.*

When my clients ask me to help them work their way out of a botched conversation or work relationship, I help them re-create the conversations that went awry. Without fail, these conversations are one extreme or the other. They may be a halfway conversation—such as playing a game of "guess what's on my mind" and "read between the lines." Or, on the other end of the spectrum, they may use accusatory or blaming words and exercise candor without courtesy.

In either scenario, the message the individual wants to share isn't the problem. The delivery is the problem.

If you improve your conversations by just 50 percent (I'm not asking for anything close to perfect), you can begin building your confidence and your career even with an imperfect delivery.

ASSUME GOOD INTENT

It's important to lay some groundwork to build trust and create safety for everyone involved. Everything—repeat: *everything*—you say must assume good intent in the other person. This tells them that you are assuming *they* didn't realize this was a problem. It says, "I'm leaving room in our conversation to understand your point of view." It says, "I trust you even if we ultimately do not agree." Every word that comes out of your mouth must assume the other person is on the same side and the same team.

The effect if you don't? The moment you back another party into a corner by questioning their motives—such as suggesting a manager is taking advantage of you by not giving you a raise—there is a low probability of a positive outcome and a lost opportunity to behave like a true partner in solving a problem.

WHAT ASSUMING GOOD INTENT LOOKS LIKE

Typical conversation: "Why did you change the dates on the project? There is no way we can deliver two weeks earlier. I feel completely out of the loop."

A better conversation: "I was surprised to see the dates on the project were moved up two weeks. There are some implications if that's the case that I want to make sure we discuss. Is this change something you intended? And if so, can you help me understand what is driving the decision?"

I get a lot of calls with heavy breathing on the other side. Before your imagination runs away, it's not what you think. But it's still a problem. It's usually a panicked individual who starts the conversation like this: "I think I just blew up my career, but I want to get your opinion."

In this particular case, the client on the other line had reacted strongly after hearing about a big change to the company's strategy. After hearing the changes, she blurted out to her manager, "This is a terrible plan. It isn't going to work, and it would mean completely throwing away everything we've worked on over the past six months."

She also added in these "wish-I-could-take-it-back" gems:

- "I don't think you understand what you are asking here."
- "You don't get it. There's no way we could even build that with our current system."
- "It's a bad idea and it won't work."
- "I thought I'd have a say in the direction, but you clearly don't care what I think."

It's easy to see how bad that sounds when you put it in writing. If you're the manager hearing this, you are definitely feeling defensive. I had to share the bad news with my client that she would have to do some repair work on this one. It would have been so much easier if she would have used some phrases consistent with the principles outlined in this chapter. If she had assumed good intent, some of her phrases would have sounded more like this:

- "I have some concerns about the plan. Can you help me understand how you arrived at the conclusion?"
- "It has caught me off guard that you've already made the commitment without talking to me first. It's not like you to make big decisions without my input. Is there something going on here I don't understand?"
- "There are some system limitations you may not be aware of. Are you open to explore a different alternative?"

I recommend writing out and practicing your personal script to prepare for these discussions you know you will be having. It may surprise you how many words you use that can hurt the conversation. If you are caught off guard by a conversation that is happening in the moment and you can't prepare, use this one question to help you set the direction: *If the roles were reversed, how would I want this person to have the conversation with me?*

WHAT NOT TO SAY	SAY THIS INSTEAD
This is more important to me than you. You obviously don't care about . . . Why would you . . . This isn't as important to you as it is to me. You should have known. You did this because . . . It would have been so easy to loop me in.	This is a priority for both of us. I appreciate the thought you put into helping me understand your perspective. We both want a good outcome. I would want to know if the roles were reversed. Help me understand your rationale.

WHAT NOT TO SAY (CONTINUED)	SAY THIS INSTEAD (CONTINUED)
There is no other way to see it. *I don't think you understand . . .*	*What are your most important* *priorities? How do you see it?*

THE THREE MAGIC PHRASES

Then there are the three magic phrases. These questions do more to defuse conflict than any other technique or strategy I can teach you. They are a nonjudgmental way to allow space for the other person to share their point of view without insinuating blame of wrongdoing. Even if you get everything else wrong about the conversation, these three phrases can create an opening to work through conflict:

THREE MAGIC PHRASES

1. "Is that what you intended?"
2. "Do you see it differently?"
3. "Is there something I'm missing here that would help me understand?"

Commit these to memory because in a crucial conversation they will be your lifesaver questions. They set the tone for the kind of conversation that can end well, even if the topic is difficult. I would know, because I had one of my own team members use these words with me. What could have been a disastrous conversation cemented him as one of my most trusted advisors.

CASE STUDY: A HARD CONVERSATION THE RIGHT WAY

Imagine how poorly this conversation could have gone if one of my senior leaders came into my office and dropped this bomb on me: *Hey. We've all been talking, and if you don't quit being such a micromanager, you are going to lose your whole team.*

This is likely what he wanted to say, but instead, he understood a critical concept: treating me the way he would want to be treated if he were the one receiving the feedback. He understood that even difficult messages could be good conflict, where courage and consideration balance out. He treated me like a partner and not a problem.

His approach was vastly different: "*I wanted to talk to you about something that is difficult. I want us to operate well as a team. We all take a lot of pride in the work we do, and I'm 100 percent behind the vision of HR you want to create for the company. But as I thought about how it feels lately, we are taking some steps backward. This is something I would want to know if it were me in your shoes. Would you be open to hearing some feedback?*"

After describing what he was observing, he looked me in the eyes, and shared this magic phrase: "*Is that what you intended?*"

This approach started the conversation on footing that built trust, rather than putting each of us on the defense. That one question launched us into a rich conversation about the look and feel of some of our employee-engagement campaigns. It allowed for brainstorming on how I could tap into the team's creativity and get more clarity on the desired deliverables rather than modifying or adding requirements each week.

More important, it was a conversation that built trust between us. Knowing he came to me to discuss this did the opposite of

hurting the relationship. I knew that when there was something difficult to discuss or a difference of opinion, I could count on him to
speak up. In doing so, we would be better for it.

THE GAP MODEL FOR COMMUNICATION

Now that you have set the stage for the right words to use, I want
to teach you the right model in which to use them. I've used the
GAP model (see figure 2) for many years. It's a combination of
many great books and articles written on this topic, including
Crucial Conversations: Tools for Talking When Stakes Are High and
Crucial Confrontations: Tools for Resolving Broken Promises, Violated

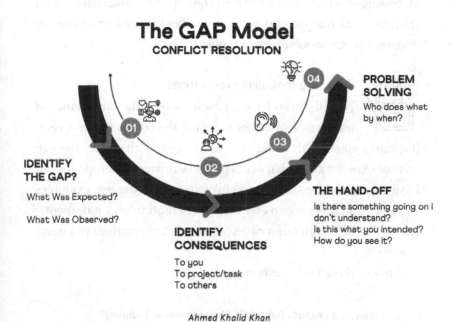

The GAP Model
CONFLICT RESOLUTION

04 PROBLEM
SOLVING
Who does what
by when?

01

03

IDENTIFY
THE GAP?

What Was Expected?

What Was Observed?

02

THE HAND-OFF

Is there something going on I
don't understand?
Is this what you intended?
How do you see it?

IDENTIFY
CONSEQUENCES

To you
To project/task
To others

Ahmed Khalid Khan

FIGURE 2

Expectations, and Bad Behavior by Joseph Grenny, Ron McMillan, Al Switzler, and Kerry Patterson, as well as the work of Interact Performance Systems. It even has a little Stephen R. Covey's *7 Habits of Highly Effective People* thrown in. I've adapted all I've learned through the years to create a simple model that is easy to teach and implement.

The GAP model gives you four steps to address any conflict where there is an unmet expectation. What I love about this model is that it allows for a facts-based conversation without the emotional extras we tend to throw in when the stakes are high.

The very nature of the first questions helps you highlight the gap in expectations, which is often difficult for people to identify but the main feature in any conflict. The icons included in the image represent stages of filling in that gap: laying out your expectations and discussing observations, identifying consequences, then handing off the conversation to your manager or another stakeholder so you can develop a problem-solving action plan.

 ## Describing the Gap in Expectations

Now that you have an awareness of the importance of tone, you can begin to frame the conversation. Creating safety starts with being able to describe with clarity the gap in your expectations; what occurred versus what I thought should have occurred. The most powerful gap statements use examples and data and steer completely clear of emotion and judgments. Know that if you can't describe your unmet expectation, you won't resolve it.

Answer these two questions:

1. What did I expect (what did I believe would happen)?
2. What did I observe (what actually happened)?

That sounds simple, but it's not as easy as it looks. Individuals have difficulty with clarity when describing the gap and doing it while staying free from judgments or emotion. Here are some guidelines that will help you stay on track when describing your gap in expectations and what you've observed.

Let's say you've been asked to work overtime. Here is an example of the statements you could use:

- "When you first hired me, we talked about having overtime work occasionally, which I was expecting as a part of the job." (What I expected)
- "But I have worked late twelve out of the last fifteen days and rather than being the exception it has turned into the standard requirement." (What I observed)
- "I would expect with ongoing work, the rest of the team would share in getting the work done." (What I expected)
- "What I've noticed is that the last four times we've had a report to get from the customer database, I've been asked to do the back-end cleanup for the team." (What I observed)
- "While I appreciate your confidence in me, I also would expect others could also help our team with unexpected work." (What I expected)

 Identifying Consequences

This is the only place in communication where you can add emotion, such as an "I feel" statement. Describe the impact this gap is having on you, but also on the project, the broader team, and others such as your manager or other departments, if applicable. Often, in work conflict, there are consequences or impacts to all areas mentioned above. Try a statement like this:

- "I'm finding that it is having an impact on how I feel about the job. I'm starting to get burned out and not as energized about the job." (Consequence to me)
- "As well, it's taking a toll at home because I'm not present with my family." (Consequence to others)
- "I get anxious when I see you coming to my desk because it's often a request to stay late, and that isn't a dynamic I want to have between us." (Consequence to work relationship)

The Handoff

The handoff is the most powerful part of the GAP model and where you insert the Three Magic Questions. Without a handoff, it isn't a true conversation. If you have done the first steps correctly, you have clearly described the gap, the impact it's having on you, the team, and/or the project. Now, in true partner fashion, you ask one of the three questions that will allow for continued dialogue instead of forcing a defensive response. Notice that all three questions are completely judgment-free:

1. "Is that what you intended?"
2. "Do you see it differently?"
3. "Is there something I'm missing here that would help me understand?"

Then listen, listen, listen. Ask clarifying questions if needed, but lock in on what the other person is saying without getting in your head about your response. When you feel you have a good understanding, repeat back to the other person what you understood them to say:

- "May I repeat back what I think you said?"
- "Did I get that right?"

Problem Solving

Only after the other party has had an opportunity to weigh in can you move into a successful space for problem solving or resolution. While I would expect you to go into the conversation with ideas about a potential resolution, be open to learning new facts that will help you arrive at an answer you hadn't considered.

PROBLEM-SOLVING PHRASES

- *"How would we solve this if anything were possible?"*
- *"I've got a few ideas. I would love to hear yours too."*
- *"Would you be open to trying . . . ?"*
- *"We have different ideas of how to solve this. Is there one solution we could agree to try?"*
- *"I appreciate the conversation. It's helped me see a different perspective. What if we . . . ?"*
- *"Is there an alternative we haven't explored?"*
- *"I'm open to your ideas or a different opinion here."*
- *"Help me understand how you arrived at that decision."*
- *"Please take this opinion as another view to weigh before you make a final decision."*
- *"Would you ever consider . . . ?"*
- *"I have a different view. Would you be open to hearing it?"*
- *"Help me understand your point of view better."*

- *"This could be an alternative way to approach it. Thoughts?"*
- *"Let me repeat back what I heard you say."*
- *"We both want this to be successful. With that in common, I'm sure we can arrive at a good solution together."*
- *"Would you be open to an experiment to try this instead?"*

Once you have determined a course of action, close by determining who does what and by when. True conflict resolution has assigned accountability.

DO THIS AND NOT THAT

Here are some additional examples of how the communication strategies in this chapter can transform the tone of a conversation. Here are some "Don't Do This" examples and suggested rephrasings to keep the conversation open and create opportunities for better dialogue and solutions.

Example #1: Team Deliverables

Don't do this: Jess starts getting angry with others in the meeting, telling the team they "obviously don't want to succeed" or they would approach the problem differently.

Do this instead: Jess describes what he expected to have accomplished on the project and contrasts it with what has been done so far, illustrating the gap. Rather than assuming the team wants to fail, he asks them, "What are your thoughts about how we can get this back on track?"

Example #2: More Work and No Raise

Don't do this: Rachel sets up a time to speak with her manager and tells her, "I feel like you are taking advantage of me by continuing to expect more out of me without any raise to go with it. I need a raise or else I will be forced to seek other employment."

Do this instead: "I have taken on an additional two projects, and I absorbed Jami's work when he left. This is about a 25 percent uplift over my original duties. I want to continue to grow and gain new skills, but I would also like to understand how you view my career growth plan and at what point I would be up for a raise, especially considering the permanent nature of my added responsibilities. I want to be someone you can count on to help the team, but I also want to feel valued here. We haven't talked about this before, and so I wanted to understand your perspective. How do you see it?"

Here is a look at some other common workplace conversations and their better alternatives:

CONVERSATION	ALTERNATIVE
OVERWORK *You keep penalizing me by giving me the work of everyone else who isn't doing their share. It's not fair and I'm done with it.*	*I'm working late several nights each week, and it feels like I often am carrying a bigger share than others on the team. I appreciate that you trust the work I do, but I'm beginning to feel burned out. I don't believe that's what you intended. Can we explore together some solutions that still allow the most important work to be done?*

CONVERSATION (CONTINUED)	ALTERNATIVE (CONTINUED)
PRIORITY SHIFTS *Every time we have this discussion, my priorities move to the bottom of the list while yours get funded. I'm starting to wonder if anything I do even matters here.*	*I see it differently on the prioritization and would like to share why it hurts both of our organizations if we don't prioritize this initiative higher. Would you invest a few minutes for us to look at my project benefits together?*
SHOWING UP LATE *Of course you are coming in late again after we just talked about this. Did you forget to set your alarm clock again or what's your latest excuse?*	*We spoke yesterday about how important it is to have you be at work on time after you were late Tuesday and Wednesday of last week. Today you are twenty minutes late again. Is there something I'm missing here that would help me understand?*
PERFORMANCE DISAGREEMENT *It's completely unfair how you are characterizing my performance. You've got it all wrong. I am not signing this warning.*	*I disagree with your assessment of me, but I want you to know I hear what you are saying. What you are describing is not what I intended.*

In each of these examples, the "Don't Do This" leads with a "you-done-me-wrong" approach. In each case, I can predict less than ideal outcomes. The "Do This Instead" approach assumes there are reasonable people working together who both want a good outcome, so it's focused on giving the other person an opportunity to fill in the missing pieces as well as finding a solution that works for both, rather than a win-lose ending.

FINAL THOUGHTS

If you are a human in the working world, you will experience conflict—I guarantee it.

Using the GAP model for communication doesn't always make for a perfect end of the story. But it creates space for the other person to safely share the rationale behind the decision. It gives a *why* to something that isn't making sense. It opens up other alternatives besides the conclusion you may have come to in your mind. When you don't understand the *why*—the intent—behind an individual's point of view, it becomes far too easy to label their decisions as ridiculous, ill-informed, shortsighted, or any number of other not-so-flattering adjectives.

Appreciating the intent of another is humanizing. When I lead conversations this way, I find that I get a glimpse into the pressures and challenges of another person's world. I come away feeling better about the person, even if I still have a different point of view. Assuming the other party's good intent will help make having hard conversations a bit easier.

WALKAWAY ASSIGNMENT

How might your conversations change if you went into them assuming good intent rather than malice? Consider some of these common scenarios:

- You weren't selected for a promotion you wanted badly.
- Your manager just changed the team goals for the third time in a row.
- You found out your new coworker is less qualified but makes more than you.

- Your manager didn't give you credit for your idea in a public meeting and instead took the credit for the work.
- A coworker has more flexibility than you and is always taking vacation time, while you can't get your vacation time approved.

Write down your own list of potentially difficult conversations. Identify one you would like to tackle and apply the GAP model to it. Then hold the conversation. Afterward, write down your reflections on the experience. What did you learn? Did it work as planned? Do you feel it broke or built trust?

8

Lies About Promotability

*Lie: If I continue to do what got me my first promotion,
I will continue to be rewarded.*

*Truth: The skill that got you where you are isn't the skill
that will get you to the next level of your career growth.*

My office was the bathroom stall.

The first month of my new job as head of human resources, it was easy to find me in my new office—the women's bathroom stall on the fourth floor. It was the floor filled with empty desks waiting for the hundreds of employees my team was to hire over the next six months. Oh—wait a minute. Did I say team? By team, I meant me and the two employees who had been hired a few weeks prior. They had a deer-in-the-headlights look upon our first introduction. I recognized it at the time to mean "I don't think I signed up for this, either."

The job that was supposed to be the best job of my life was anything but that. Instead, it was a bit of a bait and switch. I was sold on coming to a company where I could make millions of dollars in a few short years. I knew it would be a heavy lift, but I had no idea it would be *that* heavy.

It was a company that was slated to go public in six months, despite the fact that they didn't know how many people actually worked for them.

Upon digging in my first week, I learned that human resources had more nonworking parts than working parts. The most basic compliance efforts around hiring, such as making sure our hires had submitted proof of US citizenship, were not being completed correctly or consistently. We were hiring a whopping one hundred new hires per week and opening several new offices each month and yet we had no idea how many people actually worked for us on any given day. Those were just a few of the details I learned after I started.

To say the job was hard is an understatement. It was migraine-inducing from day one. There was so much undone that it was hard to know where to start. I came into the role as a senior executive. Translation: nobody is going to tell you what to do; you have to set the priorities, decide on the resources you need, and build it—fast. The company needed structure yesterday.

In between moments of crying in the bathroom, I spent my first weeks hiring some very smart leaders who could help me build out key pieces of the human resources function. We began in earnest to build. It was difficult to find time to build strategy because every day had so many emergencies. New offices, new people without clear job descriptions, new pay plans, and a new org structure every few weeks. I knew how to build a human resources function at a fairly fast pace. But I had no idea how to build an airplane while flying it at full speed. My job trajectory may sound familiar to you because it was one that many individuals I've talked to have experienced:

- The first few weeks, I knew I'd made a terrible mistake in joining the company.
- The first few months, I wanted to quit.
- The first year, I went home exhausted every evening.
- The second year, I began to see progress.
- The third year, I felt my department started to function reasonably well.
- The fourth year, I could look back and see the tremendous progress we had made.

Don't make the mistake of thinking it's the wrong job because it's hard.

I can't take away "hard" for you any more than I could take it away for myself. Jobs, and especially new jobs and career jumps, are nerve-wracking. You won't be entirely ready for the next step in your career, but a key part of promotability is stepping into the unknown. If you feel ready for the next step and aren't a bit anxious, you are probably growing too slowly! There is discomfort in growth. It's the one feeling that predictably shows up in every new job you'll ever have.

In studying the patterns of people's performance—why they are promoted or fired—I've seen that adjustments are mandatory with each new professional level an employee achieves. I used to think that if I was doing something that was working, I needed to continue doing that thing over and over. But I don't believe that any longer.

If you don't evolve, you won't grow. You don't keep doing the same things. As your career grows, you will have to change your approach. For example, as a career newbie, your success is largely measured by how well you can follow directions. But as a director of a company, you'd better not be waiting for directions. You are measured by a different yardstick.

In this chapter, we'll do a deep dive into what we can learn about top performers as well as those who get fired. Surprisingly, this data will reveal the exact skill sets you will need to develop for the next step up in your career, and it weaves together an incredibly useful map that can become the basis for your career growth strategy.

IDENTIFYING THE PATTERNS OF PEOPLE

One day as I was looking at the reports on who had been fired, I realized I couldn't answer the question "Why do people fail?" Like any human resources department, I had plenty of data, but it was general data, grouped in categories that were too broad to fully answer the question. Even when I asked the team to do a deeper dive and see if they could find some patterns, all we could see was a long list of standard reasons, from company policy violations to theft of company property to poor work performance.

It struck me that we interviewed and hired every one of these individuals, thinking they could do the job! Were companies that bad at assessing talent, or did something go wrong once people were hired? Diving deep into the notes of those fired, I learned that "poor work performance" could mean "having difficulty following directions," "can't execute," or dozens of other reasons.

Yet I still saw no common pattern to help me understand why some people were successful while others were not.

THE PATTERN FINALLY EMERGED

A few months later I was working on an unrelated project, defining a basic training program for new managers, when a thought occurred to me: "If we can build a general manager training, why isn't there basic training for people at different stages of their careers?" Was it possible that different levels of employees were struggling with a common set of challenges or skill deficits? And then it hit me: What if I took the termination data and put it into buckets by role level?

Finally, I could see a picture emerging. Individuals experienced predictable pain points as they moved up through different levels of their career! Different levels of roles attract the same family of problems. These common skill sets, if not developed, will hold individuals back from progressing. For example, learning boundaries of the job is one of the common challenges for someone in an early-stage career. These individuals often struggle with what's acceptable behavior and what isn't, such as showing up late or taking time off without getting approval in advance. It wasn't just customer service that struggled with this. It was every entry-level role.

At about the same time, I realized I had never looked at top performers for a contrasting point of view. As I looked at talent management notes and performance reviews, the top-performer story began to take shape.

People who were outperforming their peers had mastered the very same skill sets that had gotten the bottom performers fired.

The chaos of the data finally took form. Those who lacked the baseline skill sets of their career level failed. Those who were excelling at those very same skill sets were getting promoted!

Like a puzzle finally coming together, I could now see the full story.

People don't need to randomly select a skill set to work on or hope their manager has enough insight to set an accurate development plan forward. Each and every individual already has a "short list" of gateway skills that they need to master in order to move up the career ladder successfully!

Figure 3 shows a quick breakdown of the patterns:

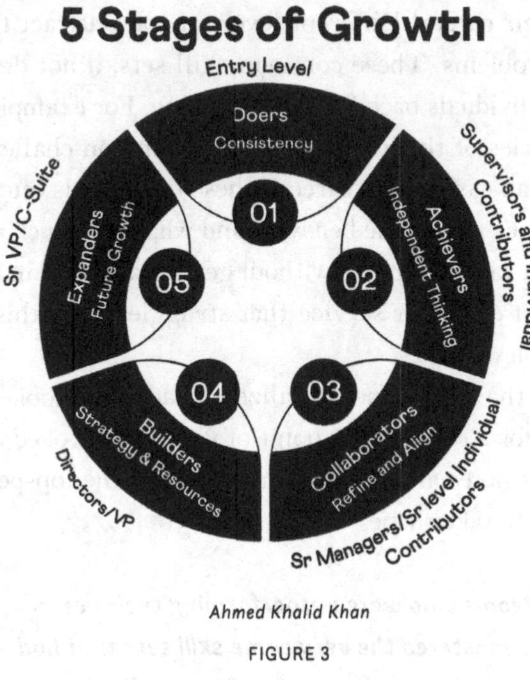

5 Stages of Growth

Ahmed Khalid Khan

FIGURE 3

While I am not a researcher by trade, and I haven't conducted formal studies, I have seen these patterns play out across multiple industries and companies in which I've worked. They have held up. They play out in corporate jobs at both the entry level and senior level and in companies both big and small. This prescribed set of skill sets for each level of growth is the key to the next door of your career.

Here are some of the high-level takeaways:

- **Early-stage careers** require one to learn to be a good follower. Success comes by being consistent and knowing boundaries. In the process, employees in this stage learn to do the job faster and more efficiently.
- **Mid-stage careers** require results and working more independently. Success comes from leading without needing a lot of guidance, strong project management, and learning how to partner across other departments.
- **Senior-level careers** require strong strategies and are paired with execution. This level requires a big shift in some complex skills like getting buy-in, which requires a shift to numbers and metrics-based proposals and better skills at working through conflict.

As you can see, each stage has a very specific set of character-istics and needs. Not sure which stage you're in? The next three chapters break each of these stages down in early-, mid-, and senior-level phases.

There should be no anxiety that you are not an expert in all the levels at once. Nor should you try to accomplish the levels in one superhuman effort. Try them all at once and it gets messy fast. They are intended to build on one another rather than be taken out of order or worked on all at once. They are building blocks, and not a singular event. Every skill set you encounter isn't like a checklist where you do it once and have it mastered. You'll have to test each skill under different circumstances with different dynamics in play.

A NOTE TO THE OVERACHIEVERS

I can guarantee there is still a group of overachievers reading this who think they can take on all the skill sets at once. It doesn't work that way. Pick one or two skill sets to work on and don't overwhelm yourself.

Consider how pilots are taught. They get to spend time in various simulations assessing their knowledge over and over. They can't simply get in the flight simulator once and call it good. It's in the repetition that the learning is cemented. We get better at a skill by using it in different circumstances, through repetition and continual testing. It took me decades to learn how to manage cross-functional projects. There are still times I cannot do it well. I started small, with small projects that were all within my control, and gradually moved into complex projects with higher stakes—more money, more people, bigger risks.

A NOTE FOR THE TENTATIVE

If you are someone nervous to take the next step until you feel ready, stop hesitating. I wasted a lot of my professional life being scared and thinking I wasn't ready. Nobody is ready.

When you are in a situation where you don't feel fully prepared, don't try to bite off the whole plan and think about every what-if scenario in advance. You don't need to know how to do the entire job at once. You are required only to take one step at a time. Take that philosophy and apply it to the stage of growth and accompanying skill set you are working on as well.

Dig in and prepare yourself for an imperfect journey and imperfect execution of the job. What I can promise is this: You will look back after the pain of the learning and realize how far you've come. While you are knee-deep in the muck, it's not fun. But there will come a time when you look back and see the progress you made and realize you were able to accomplish more than you could have imagined. Those times in your career where it felt the hardest are when you learn the most.

A NOTE TO THE QUICKLY PROMOTED

Occasionally an individual gets promoted fast. Maybe too fast. If you are thrown into a senior role quickly, it doesn't mean you can't succeed. However, you are far more likely to make more mistakes because you haven't had an opportunity to test the skill sets in different scenarios to see what happens. You will also have to absorb a lot of lessons simultaneously. It's not a reason *not* to take the early promotion, but go into it with eyes open to the challenges.

Most people will follow through a path of gradual growth and spend time in each stage—some a little faster and others a bit slower. It usually works, even if there is some uncomfortable acceleration. The key is to be mindful about the stage you are in, and to evaluate and learn as much as possible before the rules change and you find yourself in the next stage.

FINAL THOUGHTS

You've just glimpsed the Five Stages of Growth, one of the most impactful road maps for someone interested in growing their career. You have a taste of what you need to do, but not the recipe. That's what the next chapter is for.

In the next chapter, I'm going to peel back another layer of the pattern so you will understand the skills map for your current level. We'll explore the following details of each level:

- The challenges you can expect at each new stage of growth
- Your Job #1 for each level
- The skills that you need to develop (or evolve) to continue moving up
- The big surprises you won't expect for each stage

I'm guessing you might be curious about which stage your career is in, and how well you are stacking up against skill sets you'll need to succeed. Let's get to it.

WALKAWAY ASSIGNMENT

Grab some paper or your journal and do some freewriting based on these questions:

1. Without fully understanding the 5 Stages of Growth skillsets yet, write down the skillsets you believe you need to work on to be more effective in your current role and career stage.

2. As you review the themes on page 149 for early-, mid-, and senior-stage careers, write down any areas that may be emerging that you need to develop more fully. Are the skillsets different from the list you wrote for question #1?

3. Consider whether you have interpreted discomfort in a role as a sign that you shouldn't be in the role. Was that interpretation accurate?

9

Promotability: Early-Stage Careers

Lie: Pick any skill to improve yourself and it will benefit your career.

Truth: The skill sets to work on are the ones that will secure your entry into the next stage of career growth.

Understanding there is a prescribed path of skills you need to build is great news for you! It gives you focus and provides an orderly plan to develop and prepare yourself for growth. No more guessing on the right skills to pursue. The 5 Stages of Growth model (see figure 4) takes the data from what high performers do to move up the ladder and what low performers might do to sink their careers, and applies it all to a road map you can use to navigate each stage. Let's dig into each stage and get granular with what you can expect as you start your career growth journey.

• • •

5 Stages of Growth

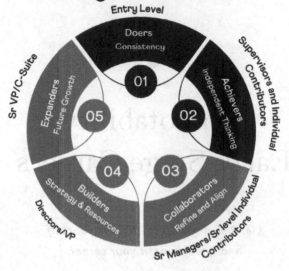

Ahmed Khalid Khan

FIGURE 4

Note: This chart pertains primarily to white-collar (corporate) jobs. These are adaptable to all types of roles and all industries. In addition to the shared broad skill sets by category, you may have specialized skill sets specific to your role, such as coding for a developer, for example.

STAGE 1:
ENTRY LEVEL | THE DOERS

Welcome to your new job! You are now expected to get it right as soon as possible. If you can do it faster or better than others, you win.

BE CONSISTENT, ASK QUESTIONS

- **Job #1:** Be consistent. Prove you can follow instructions and can be counted on to do the job.
- **What's rewarded:** Proactively keeping your manager updated on the status of projects and completion of tasks.
- **How you get ahead:** Do the job faster or better.
- **What may surprise you:** The frequency with which you will need to change or adapt. Change is constant and the business isn't as organized as you think it should be.

Skills to Develop

Be on time to meetings and work in general. For young career professionals, I have noticed a trend (especially post-pandemic) in believing the autonomy of remote work affords them complete flexibility in their schedule. You are converging with a different generation of worker who does not share your fluidity. Be on time and be present.

Meet your deadlines. The primary goal is to be counted on to do the work you are assigned. It then follows that the most important goal is to get it done on time! If you miss this basic requirement, it takes a lot of other positives to make up for it.

Keep leaders informed on progress. While it may seem unimportant to learn to manage up, this is an incredibly important skill because each time you do it, it creates another notch in the confidence column. When you send a quick update that a task is finished, you are showing that you understand Job #1: consistency.

Fatal Flaws

Not asking enough questions. You get a free pass on questions at this stage. It's expected. Don't hold back because you feel embarrassed to ask another clarifying question. It's the clarity that will help you excel and the lack of it that will prevent you from moving up. Asking questions is a sign of strength. Not asking them suggests weakness.

Not developing intelligent disobedience. Yes, this stage is about following rules, processes, and directions. But as you spend time in this stage, you should begin to develop some maturity about the times you need to depart from the guidance and use good judgment. You aren't a robot (even though it may feel like it sometimes). Follow the rules within reason, but when an exception is the right call, take the chance on it.

Making too many mistakes looks a lot worse
than asking too many questions.

MUST-ASK QUESTIONS

Considering that questions are expected and encouraged, make sure you know the answers to some essential questions when you begin a Stage 1 job.

Time-Off Policies

How does the time-off policy work? How much time off can I take? How long do I have to wait? How far in advance do I have to plan? Can I borrow time off that isn't earned?

Training

How do I learn the basic expectations of the role? Is there training I need to take? Where do I go for additional questions? Who is someone on the team who does this job well and is considered a top performer? Are there team mentors?

Manager

What is the best way to work together? What is your management style? How do you want me to engage you if I need something (email, meeting, call)? What makes a team member a top performer in your mind? How often do you like updates?

Process

Are there policies or processes I need to read? How do I track my time? If I need to work overtime, how do I handle that? What are your expectations around me logging in or out of the computer or systems during work hours?

Besides the consistency of the job tasks themselves, you are building consistency in your work habits. You are becoming someone who can be counted on to show up, follow the norms established in your department, and finish the work. If you don't think it matters, or you think first jobs can be taken lightly, I would challenge the line of thinking that tells you there are tasks and asks that are beneath you or not in your job description. The habits you establish for yourself in these first jobs are likely to stay with you throughout your career. If you establish bad habits early, it can be a problem as you continue to grow.

CASE STUDY: WHEN SMART ISN'T ENOUGH

Blake was one of our most talented creative hires. Even though he was newer to the workplace and not used to working directly in a company, he was an instant hit. He had incredibly fresh ideas and quickly became someone everyone wanted in on idea sessions. His brain simply saw the world in a new way, and it helped our company produce tag lines, creative advertising campaigns, and visually stunning marketing pieces that captured our digital audience. Case in point: he talked the company into letting him buy a traveling van, take a friend, and travel through the country on the company's dime. Who is brazen enough to throw out a proposal like that? Pay me and my friend to play! It's a great idea! Surprisingly, he got a "yes," and he began a travelogue capturing the beauty of mountains, deserts, and vistas along the way in short video clips as part of a campaign leading up to Earth Day.

It was an incredibly successful campaign. He was brilliant, except for one area that was killing him in the workplace: consistency. He didn't like the hours or rules of a company. Showing up to meetings was a hassle. Turning in expense reports was equally tough. When he was in the office, he was outstanding. But consistency wasn't his strength.

We severed the relationship, but it was such a sad ending. All the brilliance he had could not compensate for not having a strong sense of workplace boundaries.

I've seen a lot of early-stage failures. Some are due to the individual not having the ability to do the job. But the vast majority of these terminations are 100 percent preventable.

From those first jarring realities of understanding boundaries in a Stage 1, you will begin tracking toward Stage 2, where you most definitely should *not* wait for someone else to define your daily to-do list. In fact, waiting to be told what to do is the kiss of death for the next stage.

STAGE 2: SUPERVISORS AND INDIVIDUAL CONTRIBUTORS | THE ACHIEVERS

Following instructions is now the sideshow, just as you began to master that skill. Now your success is measured by working independently.

SHIFT TO INDEPENDENCE

- **Job #1:** Independently driving results.
- **What's rewarded:** Critical thinking with smart prioritization.
- **How you get ahead:** Experiment. A lot.
- **What may surprise you:** How much you don't know about the job but still have to figure out on your own. Similarly, how much you can do even when you don't know what you are doing.

Keep Your Eye on These Skills

Prioritization. Nothing feels worse than finding out you focused on the less important work at the cost of not getting the most important work done. Aligning with your leader on priorities will save you rework and frustration and naturally lead you to more meaningful wins.

Critical thinking. Moving from being told exactly what to do to defining how to get a job done is a big leap for many people. Pay attention to how decisions will impact outcomes downstream, identifying and mitigating risks, and asking the right questions.

Fatal Flaws

Waiting for permission. Holding out for someone else to make the call or take the fall is "so Stage 1." You will need to err on the side of doing rather than waiting. Yes, you'll get a few things wrong, but the mistake that will cost you is saying you didn't do what you felt was right because you were waiting for someone else's approval.

Lack of experimentation. You won't always know the right answer, but you will need to take a few risks in order to test your capabilities. The best way to find out what works is to test it. Mistakes aren't the problem. Not adjusting when you make them or continuing to make the same ones is the problem.

The Relationship Shift with Your Manager

Over the course of a career, one sees two big shifts with their manager. The first involves moving into Stage 2 when you seek high-level guidance, not daily hand-holding. (Note that the second big shift will occur in Stage 4, when you are expected to define for your manager what needs to be done in your function.) This doesn't mean you can't ask questions, and it doesn't mean that your manager is a mere figurehead. But it does mean you will need to use your manager differently. The question shifts from "How do I . . . ?" to "What are the outcomes you need me to achieve and by when?"

Your manager is now a support to define broad outcomes or projects you need to prioritize. They are there to help you understand any key dates for deliverables. They can give you guidance if you get stuck, or help you navigate barriers that trip you up. But they most definitely are not there to give daily instructions.

The best managers will help you with this. They will help define the outcomes and tell you what success will look like. Some will not, and if that's the case, it's incumbent on you to ask. If you don't, you may stumble around a bit, risk working on the wrong things, or spend too much time on something that is low priority.

Given the importance of alignment, and being still relatively new to the career world, it may give you anxiety to think about having more conversations with your manager to get clarification. But do it anyway. The risk is worth the reward.

Here's a quick breakdown of how your relationship with your manager changes from Stage 1 to Stage 2:

STAGE 1 COMMUNICATION	STAGE 2 COMMUNICATION
What would you like me to do after I finish that task?	What are the big-picture objectives I need to accomplish? And by when?
How would you like me to handle (describe task or situation)?	What would success look like in three to six months?
Can you review to make sure I did it correctly?	I was thinking of handling it this way (describe). Would you have any suggestions or feedback?
I noticed that (describe task or process) doesn't seem to make sense. Can you clarify?	I wanted to give you an update of where we are on X. I'm on track / off track on the deliverables and this is my plan to make adjustments. Would you change anything?
As you observe my work, are there any suggestions you could give me?	Could you help me resolve (describe barrier)? My thoughts are to handle it this way (describe actions) but I would like you to weigh in on the best approach.
I have some ideas on how to improve (describe improvement and problem it solves). Would that be acceptable?	I wanted to keep you in the loop on some adjustments I'd like to make to (project or deliverable). My recommendation is to (describe adjustments and rationale).

Notice the shift in language from permission to ownership. The first column puts the responsibility for decisions on the manager. The second column asks the manager only to weigh in on the decisions you have made. The first column shows a great follower. The second shows a person leading out and easing the burden of a manager without taking them fully out of the loop.

Learning to Experiment

Experimentation becomes critical in this stage, and it is this stage where you are learning at a rapid-fire pace. Some of my most valuable lessons on my profession—human resources—came from this phase of my career. The victories are memorable, but the mistakes are seared into my brain. I succeeded wildly, failed miserably, and found it to be a constant experiment of what to do when I hit a barrier.

The mistakes you make will feel big, but they
are a great education you'll carry into roles
where the stakes are even higher.

FINAL THOUGHTS

Steve Jobs famously said in his 2005 commencement address at Stanford that you can't connect the dots by looking forward. Only by looking back can you connect them in a way that shows the trajectory of your path. He said if you're worried about the future, look to the past and trust that the dots will connect eventually. That's a timeless message, especially when it comes to your early-stage career. Every lesson you learn in Stages 1 and 2, every mistake or victory you have, moves you forward in some way. Remember that no lesson is wasted—it all counts.

Ultimately, Stage 1 is about establishing competence, while Stage 2 is about taking action rather than waiting and getting results. Do what you think needs to be done. See what happens. Make course adjustments. Do it again. Get better every time. Expect it to be messy.

You'll need a good grasp on these concepts as you enter your next stages: mid- and senior-level careers where the workplace challenges go up another notch. What's coming next has complication written all over it. You get to move from independence into the world of interdependence, where working with others who may not share your same priorities is now the norm. If you thought it was hard to get work across the finish line by yourself, try getting it done in Stage 3. Welcome to the circus.

10

Promotability: Mid-Stage Careers

*Lie: I need to depend on myself if I want
to get the job done in the best way.*

*Truth: Interdependence and strong partners
are the new path for greatest success.*

I was a teacher's dream. In the sixth grade, I heard I could win a television if I won the statewide anti-vandalism bumper sticker contest. I quickly jumped into action and developed a bumper sticker with the slogan "Don't Let 'Vandal' Be Your Handle" with a picture of a CB radio on it. I won. Not only did I win the television, but my bumper sticker was put on the sides of public transportation buses across the state. (Note: I should have received an award instead for the biggest glasses that could fit on a child's face. But that is another story.)

This history of biting off big projects continued. I built a giant replica of the White House with my best friend for a school project. It took a month to build and filled her whole kitchen and took a truck to get it to the school. We won a blue ribbon in exchange for our efforts.

College was the beginning of my micromanaging. I hated being on a team where others dropped the ball and so I ended up doing more than my fair share. I may not have been able to socially hold a conversation, but teammates loved me because I'd pick up the slack.

Being a workhorse with a high bar for individual performance served me well in the early Stage 1 and Stage 2 parts of my career. But at Stage 3, my inclination to do work by myself started to hurt me. I found it incredibly hard to include others because I had some experiences where teammates let me down. This pattern continued when I ended up a single mom at age thirty with three young children. It further reinforced this whole idea of "I'll do it myself. I am the one person I can count on." Collaboration and cross-functional projects are *still* my kryptonite and I have to stop myself from taking over.

With your own mid-career phase comes all of the parts I hated in college projects: getting on the same page with others, dealing with conflict, determining which battles you want to fight, and having a voice and opinion about the right strategy. So many of the judgments about you are based in part on how well you work in a team.

It's like a college project on steroids.

Unlike Stage 2, where you were relying on yourself, you are now in a position that you cannot do all the work without relying on others to fill the gaps (see figure 5). You are beginning to interface with other departments because as your expertise gets deeper, your influence grows wider, especially if you are in a management position. Projects and problems you are solving cross department boundaries and require input and alignment. Unlike the wonderful and terrifying autonomy of the last stage, this new stage ups the ante, where cross-functional collaboration is the norm.

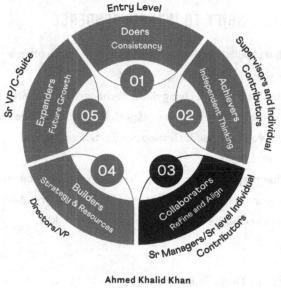

Ahmed Khalid Khan

FIGURE 5

Let me take you through what the whole journey of the mid-career stage looks like, and the skills that will ensure you can navigate the maze of what comes next.

STAGE 3 OF CAREER GROWTH:
MID-LEVEL PROFESSIONALS | THE COLLABORATORS

It won't work to be a stand-alone superhero. Independence is your kryptonite, and your superpower is surrounding yourself with the right people and partners.

SHIFT TO INTERDEPENDENCE

- **Job #1:** Collaborating and partnering well with others outside of your own silo.
- **What's rewarded:** Using data, dashboards, and metrics to communicate progress (especially as you manage up).
- **How you get ahead:** Getting comfortable with hard conversations.
- **What may surprise you:** You'll see clearly the disconnect between senior leaders and the individual contributors. You'll see both sides but get stuck in the middle.

Keep Your Eye on These Skills

Using data. You cannot make decisions on "gut feelings" at this stage. The language of business is numbers, and this is where you dig in deep. You must be able to use facts, numbers, and metrics to drive your decisions and to measure progress.

Getting aligned. Many at this level engage in water-cooler talk and blame those above them for decisions they don't agree with. There is no "us versus them" if you want to continue to grow your career beyond Stage 3. This is where you have the hard conversations to get aligned and get behind decisions once they are made.

Fatal Flaws

Acting in a "silo." The independence that got you ahead in Stage 2 will be a problem in Stage 3. If you focus only on your team, and not on how you intersect with others, you'll be missing opportunities to go faster and further.

Avoiding conflict. It seems so easy to avoid the conflict that inherently exists when you are straddling the needs of your department and those of other departments. But staying silent is just delayed conflict. Work issues out early and honestly.

CREATING STRONG PARTNERSHIPS

You will find that leading change, whether it's a project or a program, will take you outside of your own team, and you won't have all the answers, nor will you always have the luxury of getting to call the shots. Instead, you have to work in true team fashion across departments and you'll have to rely on others. It's hard as hell. But you can't be afraid to ask the questions or reach outside of your own silo.

This new level of interdependence looks like this:

- **You'll need complementary skill sets:** If you manage a team, you will need to build it out in ways that round out the existing strengths of the team (and your own weaknesses).

- **You'll need outside opinions:** You can't be slow to seek out answers to questions or problems from outside resources. You will quickly learn as you become more of an expert that there is still so much you don't know.
- **You'll rely on other departments:** You will need to rely on input from other teams for successfully executed projects. If you aren't aligned with their needs, it will create constant rework.
- **You'll need funding partners:** To get cross-functional projects fully funded, you'll often need to negotiate with other department managers to find money from their budget to make it happen.
- **You will work with outside experts:** You will find that outsourcing or finding partners to help deliver services will become important. Sometimes it's contractors who will do work. Often you will need new technology to create a full solution for a program or service.

The offsetting benefit that makes it all worth it is that you are creating visible results at this stage of growth, and you are perhaps the most important piece of the company. The single-greatest desire I hear from individuals is that they want to make a difference at work. The mid-level roles are where most of the real work happens!

Getting aligned with other departments can be hard, and you might try to avoid some of the key conversations you need to have. What makes this stage so difficult is that rarely do departments agree or see the world the same way. You are in a constant state of refining and renegotiating the deliverables. It follows that the one skill you can't live without is being comfortable with conflict.

If you can't resolve differences of opinion, you can't be a good collaborator. If you avoid other departments or act in a silo, it will ensure your failure! You can't align if you aren't working together.

You have accountability for results by working with people you don't manage and who may not be incentivized to cooperate with you. It's like herding cats, except the cats have to actually go in the same direction.

Let me play out the domino effect of poor collaboration:

- If you don't include other departments, you won't get key points of disagreement ironed out on projects.
- This will mask itself as peace until somebody realizes they aren't getting what they wanted.
- This will result in not having buy-in from the other departments on whatever it is you are working on.
- This will result in needing to redo parts of the project— or worse.
- This will result in you needing to start over—or worse.
- This will result in the other departments being unwilling to use the finished product or service you just completed.

The cardinal rule of collaboration can be summed up like this: if another team doesn't feel represented, your project failed.

LIMIT YOUR "NO'S"

It's easy to say "no" when you are working across department lines into other worlds. But when working with a trusted partner, individuals can usually find their way to a "yes" (or even a "yes" with conditions instead of a "no"). You have heard me use the word "partner" a lot in this chapter. It's because the word carries with it the powerful connotation of "we are in this together." Don't be dismissive of the word; it carries great weight.

It requires a lot of give-and-take, and not a lot of hard "no's." Tony Schwartz, CEO of the Energy Project and author of *The Way We're Working Isn't Working*, wrote an article in the *New York Times* called "The Power of Starting with 'Yes.'" In it, he said, "When 'no' becomes a dominant voice in our heads, it acts like an autoimmune disease, shutting down our possibilities."[1] It's solid advice. I've found that when I shut down the needs of the individuals I'm working with by giving a hard "no," it also shuts down trust, often ends the collaboration or conversation, and limits the degree to which I can effectively partner.

There is a weight that "no" carries with it and a price you pay if you use it too often. I read an interesting statistic on marriage from John Gottman, PhD, psychologist and professor emeritus at the University of Washington, whose research on divorce prediction and marriage stability spans four decades. He said that if the ratio of positive to negative interactions falls below 5 to 1, divorce is likely.[2] That tells me that negative interactions are a potent poison, which is as true with work relationships as it is with personal relationships.

In the workplace, we use different terminology than "divorce," but it works the same way. Consider that other departments will not want you as a partner if your own positive-to-negative inter-action ratio falls somewhere below 5:1.

You've seen this in your workplaces in different departments:

- Human resources gets cut out when they act more like a policing function than a partner.
- Sales gets a bad reputation when they sell without regard to concerns about pricing or contract standards from other departments.
- Legal creates friction when they are so caught up in protecting the business that they prevent business from happening at all.
- Marketing gets cut out when they are too tied to a creative concept that they won't hear the feedback from teams closest to the customer.
- Technology has problems when they neglect maintenance requests to make existing tools work and focus only on developing new products.

HARD "NO'S" BUILD SILOS

You don't have to say "yes" to every request or idea that comes your way. But you may want to consider moving from the hard lines to guardrails. Consider replacing a "no" with these phrases that will create openings for alternative solutions and build trusted partnerships:

- "Yes, and . . ." Instead of going directly to a "no," this phrase is a *conditional yes*.

- "I could see us trying this idea, *and* I'd like to make sure we have some good checkpoints along the way to make sure it's working how we intended."
- "What if . . . ?" This phrase immediately opens up new possibilities.
- "I'm not comfortable with X, but what if we explored this instead?"

CASE STUDY: THE STRANGEST SEVERANCE PACKAGE

I had my first manager role at Corel Corporation. When the company announced it would be shutting down its US operations, everyone in HR split, leaving me as the only one willing to stay and manage. I didn't get the head job because I was qualified, because I clearly was not. The company simply had no other options.

We had about three hundred employees and my directive was to keep all the employees until the doors closed in three months without using any severance packages to incentivize people to stay.

We were a fairly large employer in our city, and knowing everyone would be searching for jobs simultaneously, those who left the company early would have an edge in finding replacement jobs. Sounds fun, doesn't it?

This would have been a perfect place and time for me to say, "No way. This won't work." As I made my way through the different leaders in the company, they all told me I was crazy to even ask them to stay. The Ottawa-based senior leader of human resources could only shrug her shoulders and say, "Do the best you can."

Armed only with my naïve optimism, I began talking to the leaders about how we could retain individuals without offering any meaningful severance or stay bonuses. By getting past the impossibility of the question and instead asking, "What if?" we came up with an unlikely plan that saved the day: we decided that those who stayed could take with them everything that wasn't bolted down.

That's right. Starting with our top software engineers, we negotiated and traded their skills and time for furniture, computers, even refrigerators. "Joe, I'll give you the video games, the kitchen break table and chairs, and two big monitors to stay." Then Joe would return with, "Throw in a laptop and you have a deal." The entire building was covered with Post-it notes claiming televisions, monitors, chairs, couches, computers, and tables. It was an unusual bargaining tool, but a very effective one!

I often reflect upon the power of asking "What if . . ." instead of giving a hard no. I'm glad that early in my career I was able to learn there are always more solutions available than we first think.

I am a better partner every time I can limit my "no's" or use a conditional "yes." For example, it's helped me get over the hump of canceling performance reviews when managers said they weren't adding any value. "Yes, we can cancel performance reviews, *and* I still think we need a simple mechanism to communicate." "What if we create two informal check-ins each year between the manager and individual?"

Try it. The simple shift in thought processes will do wonders for your cross-collaboration.

FINAL THOUGHTS

The good news is that, despite how hard it is to be here in Stage 3 and moving from a place of independence to a place of collaboration, it is one of the best training grounds for the next stage of growth, becoming one of the senior leaders in the company.

Your next move, should you choose to forge that path, is to become a Stage 4 Builder focused on strategic planning and cohort building. Then, finally, you'll be ready for Stage 5, where your role pivots to that of thought leader, whose role is to expand the business.

WALKAWAY ASSIGNMENT

1. Identify something you have said "no" to recently. This can be an ask from another department, an element within a project, or even an opinion you were asked to render as a part of your job.

2. See if you can see an alternative, however creative or unusual it might be, that could have gotten you to a "yes." Or consider how you could have reframed the conversation to use "yes . . . and" and "what if . . ." language. For example: "Yes, these are concerns, *and* would you be open to exploring an alternative? What if we (insert solution)?" Were you able to see an alternative that would turn the "no" you received originally into a potential "yes" or "yes . . . and"?

11

Promotability: Senior Leadership

Lie: Your superpower lies in assimilating information and making quick decisions.

Truth: Speed is often your enemy and will shut down the information you need to make the best decision.

You are now a director or new vice president at this level or a high-level expert (such as a senior architect), and you've proven you can get results, or you wouldn't be here. This role is a pressure cooker, where results are on display in neon colors. There is an expectation that you can build and execute a strategy even though this may be your first opportunity to do it from start to finish.

You are also now expected to be the adult in the room at all times: you are expected to express yourself if you don't agree, choose the right battles to fight, and when you walk out of a senior meeting, even if you don't get what you want, to show a united front.

If you have spent a lot of time in Stages 1 to 3, you are suddenly one of the dreaded "them"—the people you loved to hate. You're on the other side now. Others below you may think you are suddenly out of touch, but the truth is you see the world through an expanded perspective now (see figure 7).

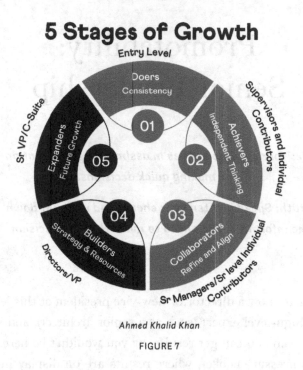

5 Stages of Growth

Ahmed Khalid Khan

FIGURE 7

This chapter will help you understand the gift and the burden of senior leadership, and how to involve your people in a way that creates greater commitment. We will build strategy basics for the new Stage 4 leaders as they cut over into a whole new world of expectations in preparation for the big move into the C-suite.

STAGE 4:
DIRECTORS AND VICE PRESIDENTS | THE BUILDERS

You can't get to this level without having opinions. But they'd better be right, because your job is on the line if you don't get the results you promise.

SHIFT TO STRATEGY

- **Job #1:** Securing buy-in and the resources to execute the strategic plan.
- **What's rewarded:** Checking and rechecking alignments with the C-suite.
- **How you get ahead:** Become an expert at giving convincing and concise proposals.
- **What may surprise you:** Being long-winded or not being clear will get you in trouble fast. You are on a timer all the time—in exec meetings and with the CEO. You must be able to present ideas convincingly and concisely.

Keep Your Eye on These Skills

Getting buy-in for your ideas. It doesn't matter how good your plan is if you don't have the resources to make it happen. Having clarity on the direction you want to go and being able to articulate it will be a do-or-die skill set.

Getting comfortable with conflict. As you move up within the company, you'll find that the disagreements are higher stakes; you won't be able to avoid conflict *and* be effective in your job. You aren't necessarily fighting, but you are always striving to get in alignment. You live in an interdependent world now and you are part of an ecosystem.

Fatal Flaws

Getting offended easily. There isn't time to be offended at this level. Too much needs to be done, and you are in a constant battle for resources. Resolve your differences quickly and move on.

Getting in the weeds. Your new role requires you to shift from day-to-day tactical work to carving out a strategy and future state. If you are a leader, you must learn to delegate some of those day-to-day tasks.

MAKING THE SHIFT FROM MANAGING TO STRATEGIC PLANNING

Having come from Stage 3, it's easy to fall back into a more tactical role. There is a tendency to stay too long in the details of the team's day-to-day work and solve problems from a micro or transactional point of view instead of a macro or strategic point of view.

Now you must learn how to drive strategy, a more complex proposition.

Many people have difficulty moving into a more strategic role (even though they have claimed they wanted to be more strategic for some time). I have seen clients who are struggling with a Stage 4 role say, "I can't get out of the day-to-day work because of the volume. How can I get strategic when there is so much to do?"

Often people are still operating from a to-do list (which will automatically drive a more tactical approach). At the end of the day they haven't moved anything forward in the long-term bucket.

YOU'RE NOT STRATEGIC ENOUGH IF . . .

- You are focused on daily tasks for the team.
- You are looking out and planning only one or two weeks in advance.
- You are having one-on-ones with every team member every week.
- It's easier to describe the team's activities for the week than what you worked on to build the future state for your organization.
- You can't list the top three objectives that your team/ department is driving toward.

Moving into a strategic leader role will shock your system when you realize the amount of time you will spend securing the resources required to execute your strategy.

Companies hire me to tell them what is and isn't working. One of the questions I always ask is, "What are the three top objectives or goals for this department?" Not once has everyone in the department completely aligned with the answers of the leadership teams. This speaks to the importance of alignment. You may think everyone knows the strategy and underpinning goals. They don't.

> *You will need to share the strategy and the plan over*
> *and over. You may feel like a broken record. You aren't.*
> *You may feel like a broken record. You aren't.*
> *You may feel . . . You get the picture.*

Face-to-face interaction with your team as well as your corresponding C-suite leaders acts as an insurance policy for success. Avoid the lure of an email to create cohesion. Take the extra time to create real dialogue and understanding. The "why" is every bit as important as the "what," and advancing your agenda will require you to do both.

Be Ready to Battle for Resources

Don't assume that getting your plan prioritized and your budget approved is a onetime event and then it's over. It's important to realize the resources aren't shifting all the time because it's fun to drive people crazy with change or because somebody is whispering to the executive behind closed doors (although that does happen sometimes). Resources shift after a plan is put in motion for two main reasons: either an opportunity emerges, such as a new product or a partnership that can drive revenue; or someone messes up.

> *The resources are constantly shifting because not everyone*
> *who got money to build their plan is fully executing.*

It's frustrating to make changes during the year, but you can expect it to happen. The ecosystem has to be balanced and rebalanced all the time. Sales change. Products change. Competitors change. Leaders and strategies change. So it follows that budgets and resources will change even in the best of companies. This means you may have to rejustify what you justified only a few months ago. There are winners and losers in the discussions about reprioritizing resources, and your projects are never 100 percent safe.

At this level there is no room to sit back. Making proposals and fighting to keep resources is part of the regular job.

> *If you don't champion for what you need,*
> *you won't get what you need.*

The quiet ones tend to get squeezed out because they don't get the resources they need. Not even the best work ethic in the world can make up for a half-resourced plan. The ones who learn how to make compelling proposals, and can articulate their needs clearly and concisely, earn their place and capture the attention of the C-suite—the next and final step in the Five Stages of Growth.

STAGE 5: SENIOR VICE PRESIDENTS AND C-SUITE | THE EXPANDERS

You are the architect for your company and the industry in which you compete. If you aren't spending time outside your own function, you are falling behind.

SETTING THE VISION

- **Job #1:** Defining the future path forward.
- **What is rewarded:** Creating confidence and cohesion.
- **How you get ahead:** Managing expectations with the board.

> • **What may surprise you:** Your people are more afraid of you than you think. You'll need to create the conditions for continual open dialogue.

Keep Your Eye on These Skills

Practice humane leadership. You don't get to simply point and have people do the work unless you want others to simply stop doing the work and leave. Being in touch with the needs of your team and showing humanity in the way you lead may be the difference between a revolving door and momentum.

Inspect what you expect. The best leaders don't stop at communicating the priorities. Inspect what you expect regularly, especially as it relates to the priorities that must be on track. Wait until quarter's end to see how objectives are progressing, and you are asking for trouble.

Create a listening ecosystem. You must deliberately create an environment of open communication. Your leaders don't want to disappoint you, and they are more careful in being open with you than you think. Don't create an environment of yes-men.

Fatal Flaws

Not adjusting fast enough. You are used to making decisions that have turned out well, or you wouldn't be at this level. But don't let your ability to choose a direction and go hold you back from making necessary course adjustments.

Being too inwardly focused. Many a leader at this level has failed by not paying attention outside of the company. You must understand what competitors are doing and how trends and technology are changing, and adjust as needed.

Too many priorities. Doing too much will hurt your results. It's a common flaw at this level. You will need to continually avoid juggling too many top priorities. It will damage the end results by either giving you a less than stellar outcome or wear out your people (or both).

I have worked with some great leaders in my time. What they all had in common was this: They understood that their job was more than directing the success of the company. They knew that with every action (or lack of action) they took, they were sending a message about what the company valued or didn't value. It wasn't "just business" to these leaders. It was personal. A good leader cares about strategy and results, but they also care about how they get there.

There is a deliberateness about being a senior leader that you may not feel as acutely in the other stages of growth. A new element of the job is that beyond setting and guiding the direction for the company, you are setting the direction for the politics of the company—the way work is done and what is rewarded or penalized. You are being watched. Your language—both verbal and nonverbal, your decisions and promises, how you resolve problems, how you treat people—it is all under scrutiny. Even the smallest things will be magnified. If you reward bad behavior, even unknowingly, you'll get a lot more bad behavior. You create the unwritten rules that dictate your workplace.

Value All Voices, Even Those That Dissent

While listening is critically important, you also need to set up the conditions that your people will trust you enough to share honest feedback. On that note, there is another reason you may not be getting all that your people have to offer:

There is no way to say this delicately.
People are afraid of you.

If you think that's too strong of a characterization, I could say your people are, at a minimum, trying not to disappoint you. This will often lead to conversations where your team is walking on eggshells. They want to be seen as "on the same page" and they are weighing how honest to be and when to speak up versus when to just "go with it." This will make it harder to get truth-telling from your people unless you continue to reinforce in word and in deed that you value and want other opinions, even when they dissent from your own.

I realize you got to this level in part because you could make decisions—good ones that got results. You were rewarded for being a person of action. When others didn't have an opinion, you did. When others needed guidance, you figured it out and made things happen.

But there is a downside to how you got here. Similar to the irony of a Stage 1 employee who is rewarded for following directions one day and suddenly has to learn to act independently, you have a similar balancing act. You must be the decision maker, but not before you listen and weigh in on other perspectives. Not in a cursory, nod-your-head kind of way either. Your people have the answers, but if you are so conditioned to being the one that provides the answers, you may jump too quickly to conclusions and miss the richness of the information in front of you. Or you may be unwittingly setting up an environment where your people don't feel you want a differing opinion. Don't let the fact that you are ultimately making the final decision impede your listening to the team.

At this stage, decision-making is one of your strengths, but you may need to slow down how quickly you assess and form an opinion. This is one of those areas where Stage 5 leaders come by their less than complimentary reputation of acting too high-level and missing critical pieces of information or locking onto data points that are representative of only part of a story. An article in *Harvard Business Review* by Adam Bryant and Kevin Sharer, entitled "Are You Really Listening?"[1] addressed this issue. In the article, they detailed the evolution of a new Amgen CEO who had come into the company with his traditional command-and-control style. He had arrived thinking he had finely honed his skills for cutting through the crap and quickly assessing information to make quick decisions. It had worked for him up to that point. Seven years into his tenure, a new drug that had quickly gained traction and accounted for over one-third of the company's profits was found to cause heart problems in higher doses and the resulting drop in prescriptions necessitated company layoffs of 14 percent of the staff. While he blamed his team for this mistake at first, over time he realized he was to blame largely because of his shortcut communication style. The article discusses some of the changes he made based on this epiphany: "It's not just about listening to the person across the table from you," he says. "It's being alert to the whole ecosystem in which you operate."

Part of this critical ecosystem is listening to ideas and feedback from all sources, including those below the senior team. Senior executives dismiss good ideas from below far too often, especially if they practice command-and-control styles. I've seen many ideas get no airtime because a Stage 5 individual didn't deem the individuals lower in the organization as having relevant enough information to merit their attention. I understand in part where those views come into play. When a group of executives are working with each other on key decisions with all the data at their fingertips, it's natural to think others that are out of the loop may not have the context to make a solid recommendation. But in my consulting practice, people are extremely attuned to some of the biggest problems, sometimes having a better grasp on them than the executives. Perhaps it's because they aren't in the same meetings, their perspective can offer up key insights from a fresh perspective. Senior-level people don't always get access to those answers. Often because they aren't asking. Or they aren't listening.

THE FALLACY OF THE DISCONNECTED EXECUTIVE

Executives often have a reputation for being "disconnected" from the work being done on their teams, or for being clueless about how work is translating down the line. While there may be executives who truly are out of touch, the "disconnected" label is often unfair.

When you look at the time horizon an executive is thinking about, it makes sense why internal employees often see a Stage 5 leader as disconnected from the day-to-day challenges. In order to do the job, they cannot get too deep in the details for risk of losing touch with the big picture.

A senior executive isn't supposed to know everything about how the work is done within their function. Instead they must be in tune with customers, competitors, the industry, and the board.

As the size and scope of their responsibilities grow, one of their greatest challenges is figuring out how to satisfy all the constituents with the finite time they have available.

Executives at this level do not have the luxury of coming to work and focusing on just building their function. It's a big, complex puzzle to put together. Or, more realistically, it's a puzzle within a puzzle. They are creating success in the company today, which means they have to ensure the plan is hitting the agreed-upon revenue and spending targets. But they are also determining how to expand the company's footprint tomorrow through new partnerships or acquisitions. Plus they are studying where the industry is headed and have to understand the competitors nipping at their heels.

As an executive at Vivint Solar, I had to be deeply conversant with the solar industry as a whole and not simply human resources. I had to know how to create the right human resources function for *this* industry. As a part of the executive team, I was in the discussions about where and how we could expand as a company as well. My voice was just as important outside of my function as within it.

Remember the Rule of 33

Consider that executives have three places they are spending their time: outside the company with board members or other potential partners, inside the company to pave the way for cross-functional success, and lastly, working within their own teams to drive results.

192 THE UNSPOKEN TRUTHS FOR CAREER SUCCESS

THE RULE OF 33

- 33 percent of time externally focused
- 33 percent of time collaborating across other functions
- 33 percent driving results with their own teams

You may see the Rule of 33 defined elsewhere more specifically in terms of the people you spend time with: mentors, peers, and those whom you lead. It's a rule I encourage anyone at the senior or C-suite level to follow. It helps broaden the scope of your influence and understanding.

It's an adjustment to go from planning one year ahead to thinking about a three- to five-year time horizon. You are putting budgets in place at least a year in advance. And you are creating a road map for key technologies or transitions several years ahead of time.

HOW DIFFERENT STAGES OF GROWTH AFFECT YOUR LINE OF SIGHT

Stage 1/Entry: What do I need to do *today*?

Stage 2/Intermediate: What do I need to do over the *next month*?

Stage 3/Mid-career: What do I need to do over the *next quarter*?

Stage 4/Director or VP: What do I need to do over the *next year*?

Stage 5/Executive: What do I need to do over the next *two to five years*?

One of the greatest challenges is figuring out how to satisfy all the constituents with the finite time that is available. Your best odds at doing it well will require every bit of help you can get from team members who feel they are true partners in success.

FINAL THOUGHTS

This concludes the grand tour of the five stages of career growth. As we've uncovered the lies you may believe about promotability, we've also uncovered how those lies can show up in every stage of your career.

Hopefully, you can now see the skill sets you need to focus on and bust the myths that have been holding you back from moving up through the next stages in your career.

If you're stuck in a stage, you can always turn back to these chapters to find a way to grease the wheels of your career.

WALKAWAY ASSIGNMENT

If you are a Stage 4 leader, consider whether you have been able to make the adjustment to create space for strategy and move away from tactical execution. Fill out the following daily four-box planner to establish a habit of driving both long- and short-term goals.

LONG-TERM	SHORT-TERM
What is the one thing I'm going to work on today to put in motion my long-term strategy?	*What is the one thing I must put in motion today that cannot wait?*
MID-TERM	**LEAD**
What is one thing that needs to be done to have a successful end of quarter?	*What is one thing my team needs from me today?*

If you are a Stage 5 leader, look at your week and how you are spending time. If you apply the Rule of 33, what do you learn about the adjustments you need to make?

12

Lies About Pay

Lie: I'll get rewarded at year-end for my hard work.

*Truth: Money goes to those who ask,
not to those who wait.*

I learned an important business rule from a former CFO. He said, "You can mess around with a lot of things in a company. You can shift directions, you can reorganize departments, you can even change people's work location. But one thing you can *never, ever* do without serious repercussions is mess with someone's pay." It's the sacred cow in the company, and the one thing you should be willing to fight for, given its immense consequences to the comfort (or lack thereof) it can bring to your life.

My first job as a twenty-two-year-old was working at the front desk in an optometrist's office. I remember clearly the first time I asked for a raise. I had learned a few new skills, such as how to do some of the prework for the doctor, take a patient's history, and use the high-end machines to perform glaucoma tests on patients so the doctor could walk in and get right to business. I figured it was worth asking for more money. I practiced my raise request and cornered him at the end of a day when others had gone home. He was so surprised, he stammered around and then, to my surprise, said yes.

I went home that night high-fiving myself and couldn't believe it had worked. The experience taught me early on that you can't get what you don't ask for.

Fast-forwarding twenty years, I've learned these pay principles as well. I wish I had known them sooner:

- Money goes to those who ask, not to those who wait.
- Companies expect you to negotiate.
- Nobody is going to care about your pay more than you.
- The real benefit isn't the amount of the raise, but in the compound effect of the raise over time.

Pay isn't everything, but it's close. The paycheck you bring home is your own personal scorecard. The number on the bottom of that check can leave you feeling that you are making a good trade-off for your time and energy. Or the opposite can be true, and the number on that stub is a reminder that you've made a bad deal given the toll the workplace exacts from you.

Think of pay as a transaction formula: your time and effort must feel equal to the paycheck you bring home.

If it doesn't feel like a balanced transaction, it shouldn't work for you. An unbalanced transaction, where you are giving too much for the pay you receive, means it's time to act.

Despite how important money is to individuals, I am stunned at how little people understand about what they are giving up by not negotiating their pay. The impact to your life is astounding!

The compounding returns of your salary are every bit as important as compound interest is to your investment portfolio: the sooner you begin investing and saving, the bigger the returns are on the back end.

THE DIFFERENCE $5,000 CAN MAKE

Although I've always taught how important this principle is, it wasn't until I stumbled upon Ben LeFort's website, Making of a Millionaire, that I was able to see it in terms that are unforgettable.

Let me share with you why you need to care about advocating for your pay—whether it's in negotiating for a job offer or a raise.

BEN LEFORT ON THE DIFFERENCE $5,000 CAN MAKE OVER THE COURSE OF A CAREER

Courtesy of Ben LeFort,
"How to Manage Money as a Young Professional"[1]

Let's compare the difference in lifetime earnings of two 25-year-old workers.

The first has a starting salary of $50,000

The second has a starting salary of $55,000

If they each received a 3% raise per year, after 40 years, the person who started with a $55,000 salary would make $377,000 more [in lifetime earnings] than the person who started out earning $50,000."

The $5,000 difference in starting salary over forty years would account for about $200,000 of that difference. We can call this the "simple difference." The remaining $177,000 difference is the effect of compounding returns. For many people, $377,000 is about the price of their house and already a pretty huge difference in lifetime earnings.

LeFort draws a conclusion I wholeheartedly agree with: the more you can focus on increasing your salary in the early years of your career, the better off you will be.

THE COST OF WAITING

Even if you aren't early in your career, the small increases in your pay still add up to enormous differences in your lifetime earnings. Looking at raises in a one-dimensional way—such as how they can help you meet your budget for the month—is just the beginning of the equation. A $5,000 raise is great, but what it does to create a higher starting point of pay for every single future raise you get should excite you a lot more. When you begin stacking twenty, thirty, or forty years' worth of raises from a rate of pay you negotiated higher early in your career, it grows like a multi-level marketing scheme on steroids.

If you are tempted to ignore this advice until later in your career when you are "more stable," it's like burning dollar bills. Playing catch-up isn't nearly as much fun as doing it right from the beginning.

There is another pay area that people tend to accept rather than take a more aggressive approach with: the annual performance review cycle. Let's take an individual who has a bad strategy of waiting for year-end reviews each year to increase their pay and they receive the standard solid performer increase of 2 percent.

Let's compare this to a person who is actively getting 5 percent increases year after year. (Note: these are very conservative numbers, and in real life, the increases wouldn't be that even. Some years would be bigger increases, and some years would be smaller.)

To make it even more interesting, let's start both people at the same low wage right out of college. I'm not modeling a high-wage job because I want you to see what this means in a modest scenario. Let's begin with the assumption of someone entering the workforce at $40,000 at age twenty-eight (see figure 8).

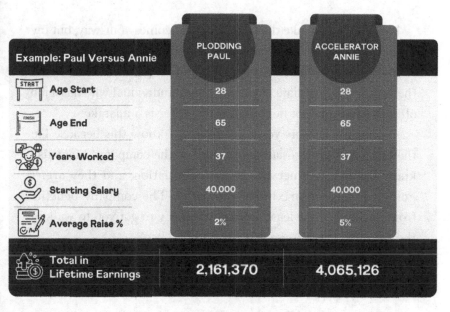

Example: Paul Versus Annie	PLODDING PAUL	ACCELERATOR ANNIE
Age Start	28	28
Age End	65	65
Years Worked	37	37
Starting Salary	40,000	40,000
Average Raise %	2%	5%
Total in Lifetime Earnings	2,161,370	4,065,126

Ahmed Khalid Khan

FIGURE 8

If Annie decided to use some of my strategies and change companies a few times—getting a few additional bigger increases—her lifetime earnings have the capacity to increase by almost two million dollars.

I don't know about you, but the amount in extra potential life-time earnings is impactful to me. This is based on simple math with base pay increases; it doesn't even factor in the inevitable big-step promotions and associated pay jumps a person would get over their career.

> *Don't tell me negotiating your pay is too hard*
> *unless you want to explain why having more than*
> *$1 million less at the end of your career is a good idea.*

It's tempting to take the first offer that comes your way, but my experience is that a company has come to expect negotiation as a part of the process and not a deal killer. It may feel difficult to find the courage to negotiate pay if you are an individual who has a job offer in hand. But not negotiating that offer is a mistake.

A company expects you to negotiate! I know this because I'm the one who has negotiated on behalf of the company. They also know that you are nervous about negotiation, and they aren't going to help you maximize your offer. The company benefits from paying you the least amount of money to get you to walk in the door. It's your discomfort holding you back.

You likely have a whole bunch of made-up messages about what is going to happen:

- "The company will revoke the offer."
- "They will label me as a disruptor before I start."
- "I will sound selfish."
- "I'll get in the door and ask for more later."
- "If I just focus on doing the job, they will reward my hard work naturally."

My question to you is this: Is it worth being uncomfortable occasionally to advocate for yourself and get gains like these? Increases for you above the company baseline don't happen naturally. To get more, you have to do something special or advocate for yourself. If you wait for the company to do it, you may make some great gains once in a while, but you are giving away future security when you sit still and say nothing.

Even if you don't characterize yourself as money-driven, it shouldn't stop you from caring enough about your financial future to at least make a run at pay negotiation in your next offer. I would never leave the important topic of your pay up to someone else to decide.

There is a happy medium where effort matches pay, and where your needs are met without selling your soul. Whether you are willing to give more to get more is up to you. Regardless of where you fall on the spectrum, not advocating for yourself will extract the biggest cost to your career.

> *Nobody will take care of you and advocate for you more than you. And if you're not out there getting that money, you can bet your PTO that someone else is.*

WHO IS GETTING THE MONEY?

People falsely believe that if they just do their job well and get to the year-end appraisals, something magical will happen. This is a flawed path because everyone is waiting in the same line for the same magic. If you could see who is getting the money and how they are going about it, it would change your pay-increase strategy forever.

Those who aren't active participants in their pay aren't getting the rewards—or at least they aren't getting the kinds of rewards they could be getting if they were more proactive. That's not to say that companies don't see and reward their top talent, because I think many companies are very mindful about this, especially in today's environment. However, it's not the top 5 percent I'm worried about. It's those of you who are continually doing excellent work in positions not as visible to company leadership or who may not have a manager actively advocating for you. It's those of you who are making things run in your companies but aren't sure how to call attention to your work and the difference it's making.

If you see yourself as one of these people, you may be waiting each year to be recognized and rewarded per your annual merit cycle. Let me open the doors to what you do not see in your company: Individuals are lobbying for increases all year long. Human resources and managers do not like this, by the way, and will push in the other direction to keep increases within the annual cycle.

For decades in my official role in human resources I've told people they have to wait until year-end to discuss increases. But that doesn't change the fact that people are getting increases outside of the company programs. Now that I'm working for you, and not the company, it's essential you know how pay works behind closed doors.

THE TRUTH BEHIND PAY INCREASES

There are three primary ways to get a meaningful increase:

1. Move to a new company.
2. Leverage another offer for a counteroffer at their current company.
3. Create a compelling ask for an out-of-cycle increase.

Here's what I find holds individuals back from employing one of these tactics: *Taking action is uncomfortable.* There is no way around the discomfort. Looking for a new job is uncomfortable. Lobbying your manager for an increase is nerve-wracking, especially when the unwritten company rules say the right time to ask is only once a year.

This discomfort is inevitable, but necessary. When you seek another job, you risk finding out whether it's a fit for you and whether you will like it. Negotiating a counteroffer with your current company will burn some bridges with the company you don't select, and it will leave most individuals with an uncomfortable feeling for a short period. But these are the moves you may need to make to realize a significant increase in your pay rate.

Remember: Your manager is aligned with the company to spend as little money as possible to run the function. They will not be motivated to spend any more on you than they feel they have to. That means it's up to you to create the compelling argument based on how you add value.

Because of the discomfort of asking for a raise, it becomes vitally important to do it in a way that stacks the odds in your favor and creates the least amount of risk. Know this: The individuals who do the homework to put together a proposal with the right elements, go to the effort of making the actual ask, and then follow up to get an answer are the ones who are coming out ahead. They don't come out ahead every single time, but sometimes those asks that get turned down become the seeds for a pay increase or promotion down the road.

A "no" isn't a loss!

Even a "no" is a win of sorts because early conversations put the stake in the ground. They make it clear what you expect and why. Those critical conversations have an impact even if they live only in your manager's subconscious thoughts. They have an impact by putting you in an invisible queue for future raises. You've essentially created an expectation that will weigh into future decisions and prioritization for money, especially if it's a tight labor market where keeping talent is a high priority. It's the first step toward creating a reality that needed a starting point and a bit of momentum. The ask is the oxygen needed to start bringing it to life. More on how to ask effectively is coming in the next chapter.

KNOWING YOUR ODDS

Let me give you a glimpse at the view from where I sit. At one company where I worked, I reviewed two years of raises given during the annual review cycle and compared them to raises given outside of that window. An increase could take the form of a bonus, a raise in base pay, an hourly wage increase, and sometimes even an out-of-cycle equity grant. The numbers confirmed what

I always knew: the biggest increases came out of cycle and were almost exclusively driven by the employee making the ask.

Employees who asked outside the
annual pay cycle got more.

Roughly 80 percent of those increases *exceeded 5 percent.*

Then I compared the increases that were given during the annual review process—the place where everyone is nicely waiting in line to get their reward. Even in the biggest departments where managers arguably had the most flexibility to move the budget around and give some significant increases, all but a few got the standard annual increase.

Employees who received increases during the
annual review cycle got less. Roughly 80 percent
of those increases were below 5 percent.

I hope that insight stops you dead in your tracks for a minute. The odds of getting more out of cycle were indisputable.

It's not only the fact that someone received the increase but also the amount of increase that is significant. In my decades of experience, I have yet to hear an employee ask for a midyear increase of 3 percent, which is the all-too-often average increase during the annual review cycle.

Almost every out-of-cycle increase
request is for 10 percent or more.

Interestingly, while the odds are stacked in the favor of those who advocate for themselves, very few people actually ask out of cycle. In today's shifting business climate, more employees are asking for increases, but many do not. I believe it has to do with avoiding potential conflict more than any other reason. But with odds like I showed you for getting a bigger increase, it strikes me as a good bet for any individual who has a good value-based argument to make. (Note: human resources hates out-of-cycle increases and will always push to wait until year-end.)

I realize this isn't a scientific result. But as I think back on my history of running human resources organizations over the past twenty years, I can say that this is a directionally correct number. I hope it makes you stop and think about how many times in your career you've asked for more.

ASKING FOR A RAISE "OUT OF CYCLE"

It is equally important to understand who is successful in asking and why. It isn't "just because" they wanted a raise. That strategy doesn't work. They ask based on a combination of these factors:

- They received a competing offer.
- They absorbed significant additional job responsibilities that are now permanent.
- They hold internal pay equity information that suggests they were paid significantly lower than another employee in the same role (introducing the risk of discrimination to human resources).
- They are part of a restructuring that is deserving of a rescoping of the role and its compensation range.
- They have achieved extraordinary results that can be measured.

As irritating as it is for an individual to go to all the effort to get a competing offer, let me explain why that is such an effective strategy. Appraising an individual's value in the workforce is a very difficult proposition. There isn't an exact amount that is universally fair to pay any given job title. There are too many variables. Therefore, companies do their best to determine competitive pay through salary surveys or other data, but it's more of an art than a science. The best way to appraise worth is similar to how you appraise a house. One of the best indicators of home value is to see what other houses have sold for. When you have other competitive offers or bids on a home, it sets its value in the market. The more unlike other homes, the more difficult it is to appraise. The same is true for employees. The best way to establish value is to see competitive offers.

Unfortunately, there is a downside to companies when they wait for this outside appraisal. Often when an individual goes to the effort of getting another offer, they choose to leave because their company didn't pay them more before they went to these extra lengths. It's a maddening reality. However, I can't dispute the effectiveness of this strategy for an individual.

Sometimes other companies aren't willing to give an increase, and the individual finds that they are paid competitively where they are. In that case, it's a benefit to the individual either way. If you get a competing offer, you have leverage. If you don't, you can rest easier (and probably increase your satisfaction at work) knowing you are paid fairly.

FINAL THOUGHTS

Now that you realize you don't have to wait for a raise, and you see there is another path, let me bring you back down again. You don't get a raise solely because you want one. You aren't owed an increase because you haven't had one for a few years, or even because you work hard. You get one when you can articulate that the value you bring warrants an increase.

Your results give you leverage. And leverage is everything when it comes to pay.

WALKAWAY ASSIGNMENT

Think about how many times you have negotiated your pay package, whether through a job offer or a raise request. Are you someone who lets the company have all the say in your pay, or do you actively negotiate on behalf of yourself?

- Write down the last two raises you received.
- Write down whether you pushed back, and if so, what did you ask for?
- In hindsight, what would you have asked for? Were there lost opportunities?

13

Lies About Leverage

Lie: The company has all the power in a pay negotiation.

*Truth: If you understand leverage, you can balance
out the power in your pay negotiations.*

The way people ask for raises or negotiate pay is a lot like how
I tried to get access to our Country Squire station wagon as
teenager.

As a surly sixteen-year-old, I could not understand why my
parents would not allow me to use the car more frequently. It sat
in the garage despite me having a list of at least ten places I
wanted to go at any given time. Regardless of whether that car
was sitting in the garage, I still only got one yes for every five
times I asked to use it. It was such an easy argument in my mind:
I should be able to drive the car if it wasn't in use. I had a license,
and I knew how to drive. What else even mattered?

My parents (whom I felt were obviously out of touch) believed
I would get too comfortable with my car rights and become more
careless with unlimited usage. To minimize risk, they wanted to
limit where I went, how far I drove, and who was with me. They

wanted to increase usage slowly, so that as my driving skills got better—such as driving in the dark, merging, having distractions with friends in the car—I would be safe.

I made a mistake that people make when they negotiate. I continued to make my pitches from my point of view: "But it's not fair. I deserve to take the car. I'm a great steward of the car."

If I had approached my argument from a parent's point of view, I would have had higher odds of getting a yes. If I had aligned myself to their perspective, my proposal to take the car would have included where I was going, how long I would be gone, and why the route I was choosing was safe (such as freeway time versus backroads). I would have made my ask mutually beneficial by offering to run a few errands for my parents while I was out.

It wouldn't have alleviated all the conflict, but I'll bet I would have been behind the wheel of that Country Squire station wagon with wood paneling a lot more often.

As a teenager I didn't understand leverage. I defaulted to ineffective techniques like one-sided arguments or threats, whining, or the old wear-them-down strategy.

Unfortunately, many of us don't grow out of this approach even though those techniques don't work any better for a full-grown adult.

Luckily, there are principles relating to pay negotiation (or other asks of the company) that do create the right backdrop to get what you ask for in the workplace. Using the concept of "leverage," a powerful but sometimes fuzzy principle, you can learn to identify the levers in your court to make a more compelling ask.

In this chapter, I'll show you how pay negotiations work behind closed doors, from entry-level positions to the CEO. The goal? Walk away knowing how to negotiate for what you want at work with more confidence.

UNDERSTANDING LEVERAGE

"Leverage" is the most important word you can understand if you want to maximize your compensation package. Simply said, it is the ability to help or harm the other party.

Leverage means "I've got what you need."

Or said another way: Do you have something that the other party wants? Because if you do, you have leverage. Here are some examples:

- You want pay and a job. The company has both. That's leverage for the company.
- The company knows the pay range and how high they are willing to pay, but you don't. That is leverage for the company because it's the ability to help or harm you.
- The company knows the other people interviewing and who are the strongest candidates. That's information you don't have. One more point for company leverage.

I could go on and on. There are many ways the company goes into a negotiation having loads of leverage. But it isn't as one-sided as you may think. You have all kinds of leverage you may not be aware of. For example:

- The company needs to increase sales by 20 percent. You have a demonstrated track record of hitting 120 percent of sales quota at your last three companies. You have leverage.

- A social media giant has a strategy to introduce short-form video sales to its platform and you are one of only about a dozen experts in the country. You have leverage.
- Three team members just left your team, and it has only two of you left with the knowledge and know-how to do the job. You have hella leverage.

Most of what you will use is called "positive leverage," which is like dangling the right carrot at the right time. Highlighting the positive outcomes the other party gets is usually the best approach in pay negotiations. In the best negotiations, there doesn't need to be a winner and a loser.

Negative leverage, the other way to get what you want, is more like using a stick than a carrot. It is saying, "Here is the trouble I can cause you." Obviously, use this with caution because starting a negotiation by backing the other party into a corner can be tough. An example of negative leverage from the company's perspective would be an employee wanting severance to leave, and the company pulling out a list of falsified expense reports, saying, "No severance for you. You're lucky we're not pressing charges."

It's worth mentioning that negative leverage goes both ways: the individual can also use it. An example would be the only female member of the executive team being turned down for a raise, and then producing an email that says, "We don't want to pay her as much as the others because she's not the breadwinner for the family." She can use that negative leverage all the way to the bank.

You can use either positive or negative leverage in a negotiation, but never forget this principle: the best negotiations focus on getting the best deal for yourself that is still good for the other party too.

Using leverage effectively requires knowing where it's found. Let's look at some of the most common ways to find it. As a reminder, the starting point is this: "What does the other party want and how could I help (or hurt) them?"

Demonstrable Results

Are you someone who has shown you can impact the company results? If you can point to a track record of getting work done that saves money, improves processes, or brings in more revenue, you help the company achieve Job #1. This is why metrics are so important for you to track. Data that you make a difference equates to leverage.

Competitive Job Offer

This is one of the most compelling leverage points a person can have to increase their pay. It is a proof point of market value for you, taking you from something "squishy" based on imperfect comp data to a very precise number. With competing offers, another company can take you and your skills and your current company is left to start over knowing they will likely have to pay this higher amount to a new hire, and the company will have lost traction as they retrain.

Specialized Knowledge or Know-How

Do you have a specialized skill that is hard to find, or do you know how to run parts of a process others are not trained to run? An example would be an individual who is the only one familiar with the CRM software that tracks sales leads. This person has leverage, because if they leave, the company will have a big problem on its hands.

Compelling Value Proposition

For individuals interviewing, this is especially important. This is how you market yourself to the company. If you can create a clear product offering (with *you* as the product) and share how you can solve the problem the company is trying to solve, you have instant leverage. If you can't package "you" in a compelling way, you don't have leverage. This kind of leverage is what swings offers from the low end of the range to the high end.

Scarcity of Resources

Is there a scarcity of people who are willing to perform the job? Particularly in a job market where talent is hard to find, the leverage will swing from the company to the individual. Consider nursing in recent years: with fewer resources available, companies began to pay enormous overtime to keep these professionals coming to work.

Urgency

Does the company have a compelling need to complete work in an area—such as an upcoming merger or acquisition? How about a deadline on an upcoming contract commitment with a key client? These are situations where individuals have leverage for more pay and often get stay bonuses to do the work.

Risk

Does the company incur additional risk by doing (or not doing) something? This could be a potential discrimination claim, bad behavior from a manager that puts the company at risk, or key salespeople leaving and the company not making its numbers for the quarter. You have leverage when risk is introduced that you can impact positively or negatively.

DETERMINING YOUR LEVERAGE

The more you know about what the other party wants, the better. Knowing whether you have leverage requires you to get as much information as possible about what is important to the other party. Job #1 to a company is getting results, and Job #1 to a manager is to manage the budgets and team to the desired results. This is a safe starting point, but it isn't the end of your analysis.

The more details you have on the specific needs of the other party, the better you can determine your situational leverage for that particular negotiation.

Did you catch that key word? *Situational.* That's right. Your leverage can change. Just because you are a top performer doesn't automatically mean you have leverage. If the company is planning a layoff for the role you want, you have none! This is one of the reasons I ask my clients so many questions when we plan a pay negotiation. If you want to make the best argument for something you want, dig deep on what is most important to the company or department and why. Company funding, anticipated layoffs, even any current lawsuits can dramatically shift leverage you may think you have!

CASE STUDY: NO ROOM IN THE BUDGET

I worked with a client who was a senior-level consultant at a top consulting firm. She knew that budgets had just been set for the next year for the project with her main client. She was the project lead, having been involved for three years. The client had asked for an accelerated plan for results, and she knew she could deliver. Knowing the budget could accommodate the increase, she felt it was time to ask for a raise. She thought she had all the leverage she needed. That is, until she learned that several other colleagues on the team were asking for increases as well and that each of those team members had gone longer than she had without an increase. Some of her leverage just disappeared.

But this isn't the end of the story. What happened next highlights why doing your homework can help you get a second chance at leverage.

She was sure her manager would like to give her an increase but understood there was no money left if others received an increase first. She pored over the budget and produced this proposed solution: If she agreed to take her raise midyear, it would take half of the cash outlay out of the equation. This left her needing to find only $8,000 in the budget. Because she was the lead on the project, she was intimately familiar with the numbers. She found a category where she could save $12,000 by managing the project more tightly. She proposed to her manager to give her half the raise now, and the other half after six months if she could save the money that she thought she could. It required no busting of the budget, which helped the manager with Job #1. Her colleagues weren't penalized, because they got their raises. The company kept her as an incredibly effective project manager. And she got the raise she desired, albeit slightly delayed.

There is a secondary principle that helped the consultant get her ask. *She knew she needed to find an argument that was compelling enough for her manager to take up the chain.* This concept is incredibly important and bears repeating.

Create the argument that your manager's manager can support.

You read that right. Your manager's manager. Any time you are asking for something that isn't a slam dunk—like an out-of-cycle raise or approval for a new program that's never been tried—realize it's the manager who is in the hot seat. Your manager does not have an unlimited number of "Get Out of Jail Free" cards to use on every request that comes their way. They do not want to look bad any more than you do. If your ask is self-focused, like the teenager version of myself ("I need a raise because I haven't had one for a while"), I can guarantee they will not take it up the chain. But if you take the time to create a compelling and logical ask that you think your manager's manager could support, it's worth the extra time it will take you to put it together.

So far, we've talked about leverage when asking for a raise. But you can also use it when it's about exiting the company.

CASE STUDY: THE NEW MANAGER IS PUSHING ME OUT

"If I don't leave now, I'm going to say something horrible and get fired anyway!"

This was how a phone call with a senior leader started. She was a top performer—that is, until her manager was promoted and a new manager was put in place. After five years of top rankings, she was suddenly at odds with this new leader and not sure how to handle it. "It's only a matter of time. My track record is what is keeping me from getting fired. We just cannot get along."

Her question to me was whether to quit today or send a long letter to human resources hoping for some help from them. But after talking about all the nuances of the situation, these things were clear to me:

- If she left right now, the company would be at risk of not hitting its goals.
- Her new manager had not been in the seat long enough to do the job alone.
- She had champions in the organization.
- She was in two protected classes (LGBTQ and a woman).

She had leverage because of her specialized knowledge (her manager hadn't fully learned the job), a scarcity of talent, a potential risk to the company (no performance plan, so firing her was a risk), and a track record of demonstrable results.

These four leverage points convinced her to relax her trigger finger and make a run at a conversation with HR and her manager that would give her a better exit than simply quitting.

The company wanted the problem to go away but didn't know how to handle it. They didn't want a lawsuit by firing her, but they also didn't want to put the quarter's results in jeopardy. Instead of leaving without another job, she asked the company to honor a three-month transition so she could leave at her pace and have the company's blessing to search for a job while she was still employed.

In addition, she asked for three months' severance. She pitched it as a friendly departure where both parties could win. The new manager got to continue leading the team with an end in sight to the conflict, and my client landed in a new company with a big fat severance in her pocket. A win for everyone. They gave it with a smile.

ASKING FOR THE RAISE

Back in the early 2000s, an interviewing technique made the rounds. A candidate interviewing for a sales position would be handed a pen. The entire interview consisted of one question: *Can you sell me this pen?*

The candidate was given a few minutes to prepare with no other guiding instructions. The responses mostly focused on the features of the pen: its smooth glide across the paper, its sleek, user-friendly design, or the color of the ink.

What people often missed in their answer was the most important part: they neglected to understand the customer's needs! They often did not ask the customer about their experience with pens; why they needed a pen and what was important to them. Instead they sold them on a bunch of features that the buyer might not even value. The big finale of the exercise was the ask to purchase. "Will you buy this pen?" would end up falling flat with the customer because the interviewee had never really created a value proposition based on the needs of the interviewer.

There is a right approach to the pen exercise. When it is time to make the big ask, you should follow a model used by the best salespeople:

1. First understand the buyer's needs.
2. Discuss how the product's features could address those needs.
3. Talk about value by comparing the product to competitors' products.
4. Make the ask and get a commitment to secure the deal.

Translating these steps into a raise request looks like this:

ASKING FOR MORE MONEY

- **Address company needs:** Show you know the company. Express what you know the company needs. Address gaps and any pain points.
- **Identify your value proposition:** Share the skills and the results you have achieved in those areas of need. Include any leverage arguments you have—such as, "I'm uniquely qualified and the only one who knows how to run the system."
- **Share supportive competitive data:** Know what your role is worth; you can use internal examples of coworkers' pay, other job offers, or salary research you have done. These add credibility to your ask.
- **Make a specific ask:** Include two or three elements important to you (reference the full list on page 224) and be certain you are clear why they are important to you. Give two different offer options that would be acceptable to you. For example, one may be a base pay of $60,000

with a sign-on of $4,000 and another may be $58,000 with a $10,000 annual bonus.

- **Secure the commitment:** You would be shocked at how many individuals go to the effort of making the ask for a raise, and then hope their manager will get back to them instead of following up to get an answer. Time kills deals in sales, and it will kill your pay negotiation if you don't insist on closing the conversation within a reasonable time frame after your ask.

Surprisingly, the actual part of the conversation where you ask for pay is the *final* consideration. It's tempting to bring up pay early in the interview process, but it is likely to stunt the offer you could receive if you wait. Listen closely here: You have only one role in your interviews, and that is to make the potential employer drool. As other candidates are weeded out, and as you go deeper into the interview process, they become more invested in you and much more willing to go to the top of the pay range.

If you want more pay, the last thing you bring up is pay.

EIGHT PRINCIPLES OF PAY NEGOTIATION

You may have a good idea *how* to ask but now you need to know *what* to ask for and *how far* you can push the negotiation. This is where companies have the upper hand over candidates. But you can quickly make up lost ground by studying the following negotiation elements and principles.

Avoid Ultimatums

Nobody wants to be backed into a corner. Using an ultimatum weakens your argument and has a chilling effect on the ask. *A good negotiation is compelling rather than compelled.* Besides, a fact-based argument with rationale beats emotion. Your manager will have to take your argument up the chain, and the best way to make that work is a logical approach.

Don't Change Your Ask

Be clear about what is important to you as you begin negotiations. You should be able to close any gaps and seal the deal within one or two negotiation rounds. If you don't, they will fill in the blanks for you, and it might not be what you want. You also don't get the luxury of changing your mind and increasing your ask after you've expressed a desired pay package—at least without putting your negotiation in jeopardy.

Know Your Leverage

Your leverage determines what you can ask for and how aggressively you can push for what you want. Your greatest forms of leverage will always be in this order: first, the results or outcomes you achieve; second, the risk to the company of you leaving by another offer in writing; and third, a scarcity of resources that puts company goals in jeopardy. Make sure you've reviewed the list in this chapter on leverage and know how much you have going into the negotiation.

Bring Two Proposals

We are a society that loves our choices. When you offer up two separate proposals, each of which you would be comfortable accepting, you increase your odds of getting what you ask for.

This is a commonly used tactic in sales, and for good reason: you are putting the company between a yes and a yes, rather than one proposal that carries a yes or no option.

Ask Questions

Part of creating a smart ask is to understand as much about the company pay philosophy and benefit components as possible. For the bonus plan, for example, understanding how it is measured, the track record of payouts, and how much is controlled by individual versus company performance is important. Otherwise, you may find yourself signing up for a bonus plan that has a track record of only a 50 percent payout—and realizing that the increase you negotiated looks more like a pay cut.

Free Is Easier

Anything that doesn't cost the company money up front will be easier to get across the finish line, such as a title change (unless the company is highly structured), flexible work hours, or bonus plans. Just as appealing are programs such as bonus plans tied to performance metrics where the company pays for something only if it gets something in return.

Use Data

The best arguments are based in facts and data. Know what others in the company are making for the role or have good data about what similar roles pay for similar skill sets and titles. Data strengthens your ask.

Use If-Then Proposals

Boards love these types of proposals because it allows them to put off paying until something desirable is achieved. For example, *If I do X, Y, Z in ninety days, then could I get the second half of the agreed increase?* Especially when cash is tight, these structures can be a good option because the company is guaranteed the result before they invest. For you, it's a win because this is often an alternative that can move the company from a "no" to a "yes," even if your raise is slightly delayed.

WHAT YOU CAN NEGOTIATE

Now that you know how to make your ask, you need to understand what you can ask for. The good news is that almost everything is on the table. Here's what you can ask for in a compensation negotiation:

- **Base pay:** Not only can you negotiate the base pay rate, but you can also get creative with how the base pay increase is rewarded. Often companies have caps on the amount of increase they will give a person—around 10 percent for large companies. But you can suggest breaking the desired increase into two parts: the first part now (say it's 10 percent) and the second part (say another 10 percent) after an agreed-upon time or performance metric. It's a way to get the full increase you want, albeit delayed.
- **Flexible or remote work schedule:** This is the time to ask to work at home for some or all days, flexible work hours, or a blend, especially if you have children at home.
- **Education or training:** Many companies don't yet have a policy or a budget for training but will often commit funds if the training is job-related. Ask for a specific amount each year in perpetuity or ask the company to

cover annual fees for a professional group or renewable certification relevant to your job.

- **Target bonus percentage:** Companies usually have ranges of bonus pay that is expressed as a percentage of base. The bonus usually has a target range by position (such as 10 percent of base). You can often negotiate a higher bonus percentage, especially if the role is above $100,000 per year.

- **Full bonus payout:** If you are joining a company midyear, you are walking away from a bonus payout from your old company. Many people will negotiate the bonus target but not realize the new bonus is likely to be prorated based on hire date. Never forget to ask the new company to keep you whole for the first year and add language to your offer letter to eliminate any proration. If you give the rationale, they almost always will make the concession.

- **Preplanned vacations for the year:** The time to get permission for vacations that you have planned is before you sign on the dotted line. If you wait until after you start, you'll be told you have to wait until that PTO is accrued. Asking for it as a part of negotiation is the best approach.

- **Timing around next raise/review:** Especially if you are not able to get the base pay you'd like in your offer, you can remove the sting if you have in writing when your next potential raise can be. It's often an acceptable compromise to request in that circumstance.

- **Better job title:** Titles are free, and yet they make a big difference on your resume. Consider the typical title progression levels: coordinator, specialist, manager, senior manager, director, senior director, VP, senior VP. A better title might not be worth more today but will have immediate value in your next job search.

- **Sign-on bonus:** A sign-on bonus is another great way to make up for elements you are walking away from and make you whole. Employers like these over base pay, because it's a onetime hit that doesn't carry from year to year. Usually, companies will offer a sign-on to sweeten the offer if they think they won't get you, or to make up for equity or bonus dollars you are walking away from in your past job.

- **Equity/stock options:** Not all companies can offer this, but many can. Given that this is the pathway to wealth for many people, it's worth asking for them, and it's often better than any other pay elements for the potential end reward. Restricted stock units are the best because they immediately have value, and when you leave the company you won't have to buy them to keep them. You take them with you if they are vested and cash them out whenever you are ready.

- **Prenegotiated severance:** Get this in writing while you are in the honeymoon period. It's easy to get when they love you—and impossible to get when they don't. It costs the company nothing to add it, and it's a great protection in the event of an acquisition or reduction in force that could occur in the future.

- **In-home office:** Rather than cobble together a home office, make a run at a stipend that pays for putting together all the elements you need to be productive at home. Consider asking for a desk, a computer, an office chair, a printer/scanner/copier, and fast internet services.

- **Cell phone stipend:** Larger companies have policies for this, but a small to midsize company is usually less structured. Ask for either a monthly stipend to cover your bill or a cell phone provided by the company if your job requires frequent off-hours work.

FINAL THOUGHTS

Now that you have the tools you need to create your ask, you just need to get the confidence to go for it! Truly, the only thing standing in the way of you making gains here is, well, you! Be brave, draft your value proposition, produce your wish list, then go forward with confidence. Remember: The worst that can happen is that your company says no to your requests. Companies expect you to negotiate. According to staffing firm Robert Half, 70 percent of managers expect prospective employees to negotiate both salary and benefits.[1] Asking for a 5 to 25 percent raise yields the best results, according to a study from Columbia Business School.[2] So what's stopping you?

WALKAWAY ASSIGNMENT

Take a full inventory of all the ways you have leverage. You may not necessarily need this list right now, but you'll want to have it ready when it comes time to negotiate your pay. Create a working list of how you have leverage in any of these areas:

- Results
- Special skills
- Value proposition
- Resource gap
- Urgency
- Risk

14

Lies About Company Loyalty

Lie: The company will return the loyalty you give.

Truth: You should never be more loyal to a company than it can reasonably be to you.

I have laid off thousands of people. I have led dozens of restructures. I have seen the look on people's faces after someone has given all of themselves, only to have that effort returned with a pink slip. It's heartbreaking to see, and yet I understand that Job #1 for a company is making a profit. Companies must change and adapt to stay alive. There isn't an unlimited money tree that companies can pluck from to continue funding all the hires they want or pursue all the great ideas that come their way. Yet there is an undeniable human toll when a company has to make these kinds of adjustments.

Whether you are affected by a company reorganization, layoff, or change in responsibilities, there comes a moment in every career where you realize there may not be an equally yoked relationship with your employer. The sting of realizing that your efforts were not worth the price you paid can be sobering.

I am embarrassed to share this next experience for reasons that will be abundantly clear, as it highlights that I was the worst mother in the world (or at least felt like it). I was driving home from work one evening, and in a moment of panic, I realized it was my ten-year-old son's birthday. I was on the phone with our local bakery, asking for *any* ready-made cake that could have a "Happy Birthday, Zac" message added to the top. Then I moved on to the balloon bouquet order, making sure it was the biggest one they could make in the thirty minutes it would take for me to get there.

At every stoplight I was texting friends and family to join for a short celebration after dinner. Then, realizing I had no present, I called my son and offered him either a party with friends that weekend or a crisp $20 bill to buy the gift of his dreams (knowing full well that $20 was a bribe and far beyond what I would normally spend back then).

I was ashamed that I had let what was most important become so distant. I remember dropping in exhaustion that night and crying myself to sleep for the person I had become.

It took many more years to understand that I was doing this to myself. This was not (as I had believed) the "price I had to pay" to be in the executive seat. When I looked around and realized there were others in equally demanding jobs who were making different choices, it clicked for me. At the end of each day I was dead tired. And I just kept on giving. I made the mistake of thinking if I stopped working so hard, my job would somehow be in jeopardy. There was so much work to do to stay relevant on the executive team, and no time to rest.

I watched one particular executive closely. He didn't put in the hours I did. He took real vacations and spent time with his family irritatingly often. He also made time for team-building and fun activities (while I worked till I dropped). He got rewarded with raises, titles, and more responsibility.

It infuriated me. Until the obvious question came to mind: What would happen if I did that? I began to watch him more closely. He created space for balance. He also knew what to work on that would make the biggest difference. He knew what the company valued, and so he prioritized better. He knew the drivers of the business. Rather than letting the company dictate his schedule, he perfected the art of working smart, working hard, and creating the boundaries that would keep him fresh. It was no accident that his endless energy level had its roots in a balanced approach to life. He worked hard but he played equally hard.

The contrast between the two of us was stark. He had energy and passion for the job when he was present. It was so different from the person I was becoming: someone tired, angry, and less productive than I had ever been before.

Two great lessons came from this experience and eventually I overhauled my career (the first of several overhauls because I'm a slow learner). First, never again would I fall into the trap of thinking that being busy meant I was adding value (which is a topic for another lie we will explore in a previous chapter). Second, and what I want you to take from this story, is this flow of principles directly tied to workplace satisfaction:

Never be more loyal to a company than it can reasonably be to you in return.

The loyalty you get from a company is tied to the results you have gotten lately, not how many hours you work.

Your life outside of work is deserving of prioritization,
and nobody outside of you is responsible to fix it.

The lie about company loyalty—that somehow companies will return the loyalty you give—speaks to what you expect to get back when you give your 110 percent to a company and then find it doesn't feel like you are getting anything close to that in return. It strikes a chord with so many people because at the root is where to find the line between giving enough or crossing over into work burnout. The loyalty equation between you and the company has to make sense to *you* for it to be a win.

More individuals today—especially millennials and Gen Z— are finally latching on to a more balanced view of loyalty. Surveys show that more than half of millennials find the concept of employee loyalty overrated, and it's showing up in the average time on the job: in a survey by CareerBuilder, the average time Gen Z individuals spent at a job is two years and three months, a significant departure from a boomer's average of eight years and three months. McKinsey & Company coined a phrase that feels perfect given what we know about this generation: "The Young and the Restless."[1]

I've seen it in my own Gen Z daughter. She works from wherever she wants. Some weeks it's Europe, some weeks it's Mexico, and occasionally she stops in at the office. She started a new business on the side to make some extra money. She didn't hesitate to take generous time off in her "unlimited" PTO plan. When her manager called her and wanted to set up time to talk, I was convinced she was going to be fired. Instead, she was promoted.

She found the right loyalty mix for her, and it just happened to align with her employer. Many employees feel the need for more of a balanced sense of loyalty, but they don't know how to get it without starting over by finding a new job. That's what we're covering in this chapter. You can begin to fix the lopsided loyalty equation and implement practical ways to create more space in your workday without any kind of announcement to anyone. You have more power to change this than you think.

RECOGNIZING THE LOYALTY GAP

A company may like you well enough, but it can't offer loyalty, at least not in the way most people would like it to look. A company can't promise unlimited money, a safe job, or unlimited flexibility. The best it can do is to offer fiscally sound decisions to keep your job safe enough. Even then, there is no ironclad promise. Ever.

I worked at a company where the CEO made a bullish statement in a town hall meeting that there would never be layoffs. He said that six months before layoffs. It was a grievous mistake that cost him his reputation.

I can't imagine a company ever saying: "Let's really pull back here. Give less, and let's see what happens." This isn't part of a company's DNA. Nor is a manager bad simply because they are trying to maintain or even increase productivity.

It's equally important to realize that it is not your job to give incessantly. Somewhere between the extremes of burnout and laziness is a place where personal pride in a job well done lives. It's never an easy balancing act, but going home feeling good about your contributions, without being depleted, is a directionally correct target.

Companies are designed to take as much
as employees are willing to give them.

Many of the clients I work with have just experienced whiplash from their companies. They have worked overtime for years, absorbing the work of others and continuing to give everything they have, only to wake up one day and find themselves either burned out, completely disengaged from their job, or, worse yet, the victim of a company layoff and out of work. Others, like myself, slowly give and give until they find that the loyalty they have given has not resulted in a feeling of well-being and that the trade-offs they have made weren't worth the price of the successful career.

The result is like dominoes falling in on themselves. The individual either becomes numb and disengages or chooses to leave the company in hopes of finding greener grass somewhere else. The trouble with this pattern is that it often replays itself in slightly different variations at each new company. And it all points to one misguided belief—that your company is somehow in charge of balancing your life.

I'm not asking you *not* to make the sacrifice of being a giving machine, but do it deliberately, with eyes wide open. Be aware of the return on your own investment of time and energy, and evaluate if it feels like a fair trade. If it's not, fix it.

Fixing it doesn't mean you have to get another job any more than arguing with your partner means you have to divorce. Fixing it simply means you must set healthy boundaries.

CASE STUDY: BUILDING A CAREER WITH BOUNDARIES

The most talented software engineer I ever worked with had a habit of saying "no" to promotions.

We asked him to lead a team of engineers. He politely declined. His reason was that he felt he was a better solo player. He did his best creative thinking without a team and felt that his strengths would be stifled as a manager.

When he was asked if he wanted to lead a key product redesign, he also said "no." Fortunately, it was a multiple-choice question, and he elected to manage a different project, a new product being built from the ground up. He felt he could create a better product if he could innovate from the ground up.

Before you get too concerned—after all, you just read a chapter about limiting your "no's," note that I didn't say that using a "no" was off limits. My advice was to choose carefully when you use one, which is exactly what this individual did.

Despite his pushbacks, he remained a favorite on the team. Why? Because he knew the conditions under which he could best shine. He knew to say "no" to promotions that would not serve the company or himself.

It is an important footnote to mention that he gave plenty of "yes" answers along the way. He was one to work extra hours for key deadlines. He supported and helped coworkers. He was consistent. His formula was simple: give when he could to make things better and decline when it would make things worse. He was a master at using his "no's" carefully.

And his strategy of boundaries worked. In fact, he ended up being chief architect, the highest-level individual contributor role in the company.

I asked him once about the key to being successful. He said, "Never think a company knows more about what you can do than you do."

I'll leave you with these questions: Do you create boundaries that help the company see the best version of you? Or does your lack of boundaries hurt you and the company in the long run?

YOU ARE RESPONSIBLE FOR THE RIGHT LOYALTY "MIX"

It is not the company's responsibility to give you work-life balance. Companies are neither designed nor aligned to do this. Your manager is not your life coach. Managers are wired to achieve their Job #1, which is getting the work done within the resource constraints they have been given. As long as you keep working, your manager will assume you've got more to give. The responsibility rests on you. You get to determine your limits and boundaries.

You are the only one in the equation aligned to create work-life balance.

Please don't misunderstand me. I'm not saying there aren't companies out there that care about your work-life balance. But the only reason these smart companies are taking action is because they have come to believe that this balance delivers greater productivity and profits. Their alignment to profit has not changed, but they have figured out a way to get there with a bit more finesse.

Even in "enlightened" companies, determining the right workload for you is a very complicated proposition.

People work at different paces and have different tolerances for the amount of work that they can reasonably accomplish. What looks like balance to one person is not the same for another. You are the one who must set the boundaries to create the right balance so you feel accomplished without burning out. Your manager may have ideas of what this should look like, but they will continue to give you work until you indicate your plate is full. Your manager does not have a magic crystal ball that tells them you have hit capacity. It just isn't that scientific. Figuring out the right workload for someone is a lot like figuring out the right compensation for each individual: it's nuanced. You are a critical piece of setting the right limits.

BUT I'LL GET FIRED IF I DON'T DO IT ALL

I've spoken to thousands of people, and this is what I hear: *But my manager is going to fire me if I don't continue working this hard.* Let's examine this line of thinking and do a quick reframe. While it's not an impossibility that you could get fired if you can't do it all, this is not an accurate reflection of what is likely to happen as you create some healthy boundaries for yourself. It's worth saying that many, if not most, of the healthy boundaries you can put in place don't need any grand announcement. As Nike's timeless motto says: Just Do It.

> *There is always someone working "less" than you who is considered a great performer!*

I have a suspicion you may have fallen prey to some of the same misperceptions I had before I learned that I had control over work-life balance and my own work experience.

When I ask my clients to identify people in the company who work "less hard" than them, they can always list several names. Often they resent that these other people get away with it. Do you catch the irony here? The same people who make this observation believe that any changes to their own current output, however small, would warrant immediate termination. This is an interesting exercise because it highlights that when we look through the lens of other people, we feel their jobs are safe. Yet we believe if we behaved the same way, we would be held to a different standard.

The truth is, you can make small shifts to work dedication and still be a great contributor to the team. When you observe people who are considered top performers, you may learn that these people aren't necessarily better at doing more in terms of work volume but at getting the right work done in a way that is meaningful to the company. The truth is you can safely create some space outside of the chaos.

PROVING YOURSELF

The rebuttal I often hear back is this: *I want to show the company they can count on me, and then once I've established myself, I can get back to a normal pace.* To those individuals I say, "You are creating a trap of your own making that will be hard to get out of." Starting too hard and fast is like running a 1,000-meter race at a 100-meter sprint pace. You set the bar impossibly high to maintain that speed. Pace is important because it sets the tone for the rest of your career. People who "go hard" and then pull back have the unfortunate experience of their manager wondering why they suddenly became less productive. I've been in those discussions with managers many times! Doing solid work—our best work—is something we should all strive for. But giving yourself a realistic pace will not destroy your career or your manager's view of you. It won't even affect your output if you get smarter about how you work (which we will talk about next). In fact, I doubt anyone but you will notice the subtle shift.

In giving yourself some space, you will find you have more energy and enthusiasm. It will give you fresh eyes to approach the work you do differently. But it's your call to make. If you feel that your beat and bloodied soul is the only evidence your manager will accept to prove yourself, you can make that choice. But I'm promising there is a better way.

If you think working overtime is your greatest contribution to lay on the loyalty altar, you are misguided. Your reward will be nothing except an expectation to keep up the pace.

At the end of that sacrifice, you'll be tired, burned out, and over-worked. Like my colleague who figured it out early, a far better bet for long-term success both in terms of job satisfaction and job per-formance is to make more mindful choices to do the right work.

THE 10 PERCENT MIRACLE

Through my coaching practice, I am convinced that anyone in any job can gain back an easy 10 percent of their time by being smarter about the work they do and the order in which they do it. I call this the 10 Percent Miracle. In part, it's miraculous because it is so easy to implement, and its benefits are immediate. It doesn't take away work, nor does it change the expectations placed upon you, but it does allow you to engage with work deliberately, which is the first step in creating better balance and results that matter to the business. It will allow you to gain back valuable time by prioritizing the work with a more analytical eye.

The biggest way to get 10 percent back? Get clear on where you are spending your time. We often let our day happen to us instead of getting clear about what's most important to work on first. Stephen R. Covey uses a great visual about time management: On the table are two jars. The first jar is filled first with a layer of sand, then with small gravel, and finally with rocks of increasing size. All the rocks don't fit in the jar. The second jar is filled first with the big rocks, then the gravel, which fills in the gaps around the rocks, and finally the sand, which fills in all the cracks. The second jar has room to spare with every rock comfortably positioned. The jars represent your time in any given day. The sand represents the least important tasks, and as the rocks get larger, they represent your most important work to accomplish (such as key initiatives or projects with a deadline).

Order Matters

Cullyn Cowell

The point is that you need to take time to do the most important parts of your job first and work methodically to the unimportant and menial tasks. The lesson has stuck with me over many decades. When I'm overwhelmed and need balance back, I do a short check-in with myself at the beginning and end of each day to mold my time back into a structure where I can do more by working smarter.

Finding Your 10 Percent

Let's do some simple math:

A business workday is eight hours, or 480 minutes.
Ten percent of that is forty-eight minutes.

That's cutting one meeting a day. It's working on emails once a day instead of all day. It may be creating better email habits or making meetings more productive. It may be outsourcing some of the administrative minutiae or even just turning off notifications during your day.

Stop the nonproductive work the moment you
realize you are spending time there.

Identify the Time-Wasters

You will find that you can get back 10 percent of your day by reallocating your attention from time-wasting activities to more important work. Let's identify how many minutes or hours you spent today doing time-sucking activities:

TIME-WASTERS	TIME SPENT
How much time did you spend reading emails where you were cc'd (but didn't need to reply)?	_____
How much time did you spend answering or organizing emails?	_____

TIME-WASTING ACTIVITIES (CONTINUED)	TIME SPENT (CONTINUED)
How much time did you spend in meetings that weren't relevant or useful or could have been handled differently (through a shorter meeting or email)?	_____
How much time did you spend on hold (either on personal or business calls)?	_____
How much time was spent on nonproductive talk or taking extra breaks?	_____

Identify Critical Work

Now, let's go to the other end of the spectrum and see how much time you spent doing parts of the job that are critical to driving results forward. I want you to look only at what key objectives or deliverables you are on the hook for. How much time did you spend on critical work?

CRITICAL WORK	TIME SPENT
How much time did you spend working on department initiatives?	_____
How much time was spent working on speeding up processes or adding more value to existing processes?	_____
How much time was spent on the work that you think makes a meaningful difference?	_____

Note that these numbers will *not* add up to eight hours. In theory, the rest of the things you do would fill the remaining time. As you look at these numbers, I have two questions for you:

1. If you are spending only X hours on critical projects and priorities, where is the rest of the time going?

2. Do you think the company is valuing that time spent on other work? Because if they aren't, you shouldn't be doing it.

Then reflect further. Ask yourself these questions:

- Does it surprise you how little time goes to the most important work?
- Does it frustrate you to see how much time is spent on time-sucking activities?
- Can you see a path leading to the elimination of some meetings, for example, or to putting limitations on emails, or to setting new email etiquette rules for the team that could save time?
- Is there some work that you have been doing that isn't important enough to continue doing?

Many of the individuals I've worked with have found their Miracle 10 Percent through this exercise, which helps them see their workday through fresh eyes. Many immediately find the 10 percent by making one change to the time-wasting activities. Others can find 20 percent or more that they can give back to themselves by rethinking the work they do through the lens of whether it's valuable to the company.

Whatever your solution is, it begins with an honest assessment and reframing your thinking from "All the work must be fit in to my day" to "I can design a better workday altogether."

THE UNSPOKEN TRUTHS FOR CAREER SUCCESS

BALANCE BUCKETS

Giving back to yourself is another way to level out the loyalty equation. Taking care of yourself doesn't have to mean taking a long sabbatical or filing for FMLA time off (although that is certainly an option). For most people it's the small and simple changes that can breathe some life back into their soul. I've created three buckets to make immediate changes to your work-life dynamic, each with different risk levels.

The Just-Do-It Bucket

The first bucket does not require any big announcement to anyone. The beauty of this miracle bucket is you get to jump right in and begin doing. It will give you some immediate relief! None of these items will put your job in jeopardy or ask anyone to solve work-life balance for you. On the contrary, these changes give you back control and help you realize you have the power to give yourself some balance.

- Take two ten-minute stretch or meditation breaks during the day.
- Take lunch away from your desk and allow at least thirty minutes.
- Reserve a three-hour break from work at least once a week for relaxing activity.
- Plan and request PTO for the year to ensure it's used.
- Plan at least one three-day weekend each month for a short getaway.
- Write a note to a colleague or friend expressing gratitude: consider sharing one of their talents/gifts or thanking them.

- Make a five-minute phone call to someone in your company you don't know well; ask them to share something unique about themselves.
- Schedule a webinar on a topic of interest that could help you in your role.
- Schedule a monthly long lunch away from the office with someone you'd like to get to know better.
- Turn off your phone and media after work and through dinner.
- Stop when you are stressed and turn on your favorite song from high school—at full blast.
- Assess your workload and assign tasks like research, presentations, or administrative work to inexpensive gig workers (such as those available to hire on Fiverr).
- On weekdays, look at emails only three times a day: when you arrive, midday, and end of day.
- Review your next-day priorities the night before.

The Get-Input Bucket

The second bucket contains boundaries or work shifts that may be more noticeable to your manager, and you would be well served to at least have a discussion with them to make them aware of the adjustments you'd like to make. They are not controversial items. In most cases they will have your manager's support. Although you don't have to include your manager, if you are working on creating a better partnership (see chapter 5, "Lies About Power"), you'd be well advised to at least approach your manager with some of these adjustments.

- Reexamine meeting necessity and ask to be released from meetings you don't need to attend.
- Do weekly manager prioritization check-ins.
- Create boundaries on after-hours or weekend work.
- Agree on "meeting-free" blocks of time.
- Transition update meetings to email updates, reserving meetings for working sessions.

The Big-Ask Bucket

The stakes are higher in the third bucket. This is the category that requires a few deep breaths and preparation because you are asking for resources (remember that a manager's and a company's Job #1 points back to money), and this will require you to have the right proposal and the right conversation. It can also mean it's time to have a crucial conversation about your own work satisfaction. Admittedly, these changes are harder to make and riskier, but they can have meaningful results if the other buckets have not fully addressed the problems.

- Request temporary help for high-need times.
- Ask for an additional resource.
- Request reallocation of work duties among the team.
- Ask your manager for role cross-training so team members can help one another during high-volume times.
- Explore a different career path or role.

People often neglect these buckets and all of the options they present to create more balance when it becomes a habit to prioritize the company ahead of yourself. It's easy to forget the value that boundaries can bring to your sanity. If you are feeling frazzled day and night, I can all but guarantee you are creating that dynamic for yourself. If you have done all you can to get back some time and you find there is still too much for any reasonable individual to do, it's time for a come-to-Jesus moment that I call the "Choices" discussion.

THE "CHOICES" DISCUSSION

There is an alternative to saying, "Yes, I will do the work," or "No, I won't." The power in a "Choices" discussion is that it allows you to manage your work by creating a proposed prioritization, and it allows your manager to see the work laid out and weigh in on its importance. At its core, this is a discussion about priorities and business needs. It brings the manager into a joint decision with you about what to drop from the list and what priorities to move into the lead position.

My career (and yours) will be full of projects, budgets, and proposals that are unrealistic. I've seen sales teams take on a quota with no path to success, an HR team establish recruiting goals without a head count to support the increases, and a customer support team that was asked to shorten call times and increase customer satisfaction without the technology to assist. For individuals, this usually takes on the form of more expectations and more deliverables without added staffing or tools. If it sounds familiar, it's because it is one of the most pervasive causes of workplace burnout.

Most people will take on these unrealistic projects without much pushback in order to avoid conflict. They continue to take the work given to them, no matter how unrealistic it may be. Occasionally, they knock it out of the park, which only sets them up for failed expectations going forward. As the expectations for elevated workload continue, performance usually dips, directly correlating with a drop in employee engagement. Then they leave.

Before you do that, why not learn how to negotiate priorities? If you plan to grow professionally, you'll need to be able to negotiate. It may save your sanity to learn the basics earlier in your career.

The idea behind the conversation is that you can't pick up one end of the stick without picking up the other. When more work is expected (or less money or head count is given), it will have a corresponding consequence. For example, I can remember being given a 30 percent budget cut in a meeting for one of my departments. My response was, "Of course you can do that. If that is the decision we need to make to save money, I want to be a part of that solution. However, what I cannot do is cut 30 percent and keep all the services the same. The cut will require dropping the manager training program and the top performer mentoring program. If you disagree with those program cuts, I'm happy to discuss the other programs we could cut. But we do not have the option of trying to do all the same things with 30 percent less money. The choice to cut the budget is a choice to cut programs. I just want to be clear on the new expectations from my department, so we are all aligned."

This conversation helps not only clarify the choices that are being made, but the consequence of those choices. In that regard, it is a way to align on the areas your department or company is saying yes to, as well as the ones it is saying no to, both of which are powerful tools of clarity. While it is also true that you may be able to find efficiencies that can help make the program cut not as drastic, it is unrealistic to assume all things remain the same when your funding or head count is pulled. Lastly, it is an effective way to continue to refine the priorities and expectations week after week. It can act as a project management tool that keeps both you and your manager aligned at all times.

SCRIPT The Choices Discussion Script

It is important to me we look good as a department. I want to be a person you can rely on to help us look good. I appreciate that you are trying to build a function that is relevant to the business and addresses some of the business's toughest issues. I want to be a part of the solution.

I'm running into a problem I'd like your help to solve. I've taken my best stab at it, and I'd love your opinion. The work on my plate is exceeding the hours there are to complete everything and to do it well. I have made some choices on prioritization that I would like you to weigh in on. I'm concerned if we don't get clear on priorities, our most important projects may slip or suffer in quality, which is the last thing I want to happen.

Here is how I would propose we prioritize the projects on my plate in order to make the most visible and strategic initiatives successful. I want to ensure these are done well, and I realize nothing in these areas can slip through the cracks.

I will do everything in my power to get everything done, but if I can't, I want to make sure we are aligned to the highest priorities.

SCRIPT When the Manager's Rebuttal Is, "But We Have to Do Everything"

Making the right choices will be critical to our success. If we say "yes" to everything, we will risk not excelling on the most visible and important projects. At this point we have to make some choices, and I've done all I can to be faster and to handle my workload more efficiently.

If we can determine what to say "no" or "not yet" to, then I can deliver well on the things we say "yes" to.

I know it's not your intention to want me or anyone on the team to fail and you want to win as a department just like I do. As you look at the prioritization, do you see it any differently?

FINAL THOUGHTS

It may feel awkward to make this shift, but you must be loyal to yourself ahead of the company. Understand that the company will always be loyal to its needs first as well. This doesn't preclude you from having a good, or even a great, relationship with your company. But you are your best advocate when it comes to work-life balance. The moment you abdicate that responsibility to the company or your manager, expect less than stellar results.

Furthermore, the space you create will give you a fighting chance to reclaim the workplace satisfaction you are seeking. Being aware and deliberate in how you approach your workday, and making microchanges to create spaces in your day will make a difference without putting your job in jeopardy.

Gain back your 10 percent and shoot for 20 percent! You'll be surprised at your ability to create the change without noticeable disruption.

WALKAWAY ASSIGNMENT

Create your own visual mason jar full of rocks, with the biggest and most impactful work representing the biggest rocks, and the most menial work representing the small gravel or sand. Visualize how you are currently managing your time to see if there is an opportunity to rearrange how you do your work and ensure the most critical work is done.

What changes can you make to reorder your work?

15

Lies About Burnout

Lie: The only answer is to do less or
push through the work to get it done.

Truth: If you slow down,
your brain will help you to speed up.

There was a popular commercial in the 1980s, a public health announcement intended to highlight the dangers of drug use and persuade the listener in fifteen seconds not to take drugs. It started with a picture of an egg and then a voice said, "This is your brain." The egg was then cracked, and the contents fell into a very hot pan. As soon as the egg hit the surface of the frying pan, it began to sizzle and cook. Then the voice said, "This is your brain on drugs." For four seconds, the egg sizzled and sputtered, and it was impossible not to picture your own brain frying itself lifeless if you took drugs. It was an extremely effective ad, winning multiple awards. It was said to have done more to curb drug use than all other drug-prevention marketing combined, with a reported 92 percent of teens having seen a version of the ad.[1] I remember it well. It is one of only a handful of commercials I can recall from my childhood.

Consider that same powerful visual for your own brain on work overload. It cannot operate properly when it is in a state of constant stimulation. A twelve-hour workday repeated over and over or constant skipped lunches or breaks will, over time, begin to take its toll. While your brain is amazingly resilient, when you stay in the same environment for hours on end, your brain will reach a point where it's begging for a break.

Here I am, a teacher who talks about how to overcome burnout, and yet I found that during the writing of this book, I became overwhelmed with family challenges, a business that was charging forward while I hung on for dear life, and a book manuscript that I was trying to fit into the cracks. Burnout is still an area in which I continually struggle and have to refine myself. If there is an upside, it's that I am still striving toward unlocking greater productivity while finding balance along the way.

Extended work overload has a diminishing set of returns. For instance, I can tell you after working a twelve-hour day, you should never attempt to fix a disposal with a broom handle based on a YouTube DIY video. Nor should you answer emails at midnight thirty minutes after taking Ambien. I cannot stress this enough. However, I can attest that gaining productivity is about more than cramming additional activities into your day. It's not as much about the tasks as it is about you and your brain. The brain is a fantastic machine, and it can put up with a lot of abuse. But it isn't designed to give endlessly without eventually getting something in return.

Human beings are not designed to be in a continual work loop all hours of the day. Aside from the life-shortening stress, which is the first problem it presents, it has a practical downside on the very thing individuals are trying to achieve: work productivity. The Society for Human Resource Management put out a shocking statistic in 2016: one in five employees works sixty-plus hours in a week and more than 50 percent experience burnout.[2] Flash-forward past a pandemic, and the latest data shows that 84 percent of millennials, now the bulk of the workforce, are reporting burnout. That's a massive shift of 30 percent in only a few years. If you think your brain was tired before . . .

I've got news for you: A sixty-hour workweek—or even anything remotely close to that—isn't a solution. It's a problem that individuals need to look at more closely and realize the enormous cost. If your solution is to do the same work but do it faster or longer, or to keep pushing yourself to "get caught up," your solution is flawed from the get-go. Picking up the pace will do one thing for you: guarantee a crash and burn. That's what we'll cover in this chapter—how to avoid a crash and burn and recognize what your brain is trying to tell you before you reach that point. But first, let's dispel some productivity myths.

BUSTING THE PRODUCTIVITY MYTHS

There are ways to recast your workday, as we discussed in the last chapter. The idea of balancing the loyalty equation with better time management techniques can certainly help with work overload. But there is another angle to greater productivity, and it has nothing to do with work and everything to do with you—or, more specifically, your brain. You are carrying around some very ineffective ideas about how to fix the problem of overwork. These thought tracks are making the problem worse.

If you simply listen to what your brain is trying to tell you, you may be able to do more without necessarily giving more.

Myth 1: *If I Push Hard, I Can Get "Caught Up"*

Thinking you will get caught up if you work longer is nothing but a mirage that moves farther away every time you think you are getting close. It's a bad strategy if you are using it for extended periods of time because it creates a pattern you might not even be aware of. Working harder was my go-to strategy for many years. Until it became my habit and I forgot I was even doing it.

Playing catch-up is the first thing most people do when the work begins to pile up. We think if we keep at it, and make a big final push, we will eventually hit the "work-slows-down" pot of gold at the end of the rainbow. But more times than not, there's no gold. There isn't even a pot. There's just more work. Yet we continue to operate as though one last push will fix it. It rarely does.

Myth 2: *If I Change Jobs, It Will Get Better*

It's easy to make the mistake of thinking the only way to "cure" overwork is by making big, sweeping changes like leaving your job. While starting over can provide some relief, I find that it's often temporary, and the strategy fails because the problem starts with you and your boundaries. One of my deepest-held beliefs about people in the workforce is that they want to make a difference. When an individual gets caught in an endless loop of overwork, and they aren't equipped with better strategies and tools, they eventually disengage.

Leaving a job, particularly if work overload started the whole chain of events, doesn't usually solve the problem long term. In the short term, individuals start with high hopes when they talk to a company that touts their commitment to work-life balance. Sometimes a person gets lucky and does find a job with better balance built in. But my experience is that the familiar pattern often repeats itself, even if it takes some time to show up again. When the individual starts a new job, they try to prove themselves for the first several months. As they gain their manager's confidence, they get more work to do. To the person who felt they didn't make a difference at the old company, feeling needed again feels wonderful. It would be great if it stopped there. But a direct correlation to being a top performer is getting more responsibility. We are conditioned easily then into doing more because there is an intrinsic reward. A year into the new job, don't be surprised if the same problem is re-created at the new company. Wherever you go, there you are.

If you struggle with setting the right boundaries or continue to solve overwork in the same ineffective ways, you'll contribute to your own burnout wherever you go.

I'm not saying that this is all your fault. There is plenty of blame to go around between the company, your manager, and even you for work overload. I am also not naïve enough to suggest that changing companies is a bad answer every time, because it can be a good strategy. But often individuals fail to see their own patterns and how they add to the problem when it reemerges. You have to be self-aware of your go-to patterns (such as *I'll just work harder till I'm caught up*) and break your own bad habits if you expect to change your experience.

Myth 3: *If I'm Doing Too Much, the Answer Is to Do Less*

Instead of thinking you should push, push, push to get more done, you might conversely think that you should just do less. Sounds logical enough. Taking work off your plate may seem like the first thing you should do if you find yourself out of balance. Although work allocation is a part of the solution, it is a gross oversimplification to decide the best or only solution is to simply do less.

What if I told you that you could be more productive if you stopped the push and pull and allowed your brain some time to work its magic? There are many ways to fix burnout besides pushing yourself to catch up, leaving your job, or taking work off your plate. *When* and *how* you do work becomes an incredibly important part of the equation. Understanding what we know about how our brains work will help you work with and not against yourself.

WHAT YOUR BRAIN IS TRYING TO TELL YOU

It's helpful to understand the brain and how it behaves under stress. The most highly evolved human computer that has ever existed—the very organ that is genius enough to figure out how to send a man to the moon or build the pyramids of Egypt—is telling you what to do each and every day about overload.

When your brain gets tired, it stops working well. It actually slows down its processing of information and crawls along until it can refresh itself. Paradoxically, less is more. Breaks from overfocusing are as essential to the brain as oxygen is to staying alive. Working intermittently increases your odds of achieving what you are trying to achieve, and working harder and longer, especially for extended periods of time, decreases the odds of success. Your brain can't be any clearer in telling you what you need to do.

The very thing you think will solve the problem is exacerbating it and all but guaranteeing your failure! You can push yourself over and over, but you'll see that there are diminishing returns. What you can get done and the quality of that work goes down even though you are giving it more attention. Pulling back and giving your brain more down time, or allowing it other areas of relaxation or pleasure—even if it's just taking a lunch hour—will increase your work output. The very thing that can save you from overload is the one thing most people avoid. We skip breaks, we work through our lunch hour, and work long after we should be "off." Trying to catch up is actually slowing you down.

When you continuously work through your day without breaks, you are breaking your brain.

If you've ever been so burned out that all you can do is stare at your computer or you find that all you've accomplished in an hour is mustering up the effort to answer emails, your brain is responding to overstimulation. It's short-circuiting until it can shift to another file folder and preferably something not as intense. When this happens, your brain could not be any clearer: *I am shutting down until I can recharge. You can keep going if you want, but I am shutting down and you will be going at it alone.*

Instead of listening, we push ourselves harder and further, expecting our brain will suddenly turn on again and leap into action if we show it who is boss. It doesn't work that way. We don't get to boss our brains around for hours, days, weeks, or months at a time. While you may be able to push yourself sometimes for an important assignment or deliverable, you can't expect to abuse your brain every day and think you will get the results you want.

You cannot bully your brain.

While the brain is an amazing organ and can soak up a lot of information, there comes a saturation point where a pivot is

required. Meditation teacher Michael Taft calls it "cerebral congestion," a perfect visual term to describe what it feels like when
we are burned out from too much work without a break.

Your version of cerebral congestion may feel like one of these
complaints I commonly hear:

- "I know there is so much work to do, but I'm getting
  less and less done the harder I try."
- "I feel like a robot. I have no emotion attached to the
  work I do anymore. I've lost the personal pride I once
  had in my work quality."
- "Sometimes I feel completely incapable of doing the hard
  parts of my job and find I've been answering old emails
  for hours without accomplishing anything of substance."
- "I looked at what I got done at the end of the day and I
  worked hard, but I can't see that I really did any work
  that was worthwhile. It's so frustrating."

The cure for brain overwork has been scientifically proven
many times over. Surprisingly, it's fairly simple: slow down. The
very act of slowing down will allow you to go faster in the end.

Create brain rest times. Pivot into something pleasurable or
different. Doing so, even in small spurts, actually increases overall
productivity and our ability to process information when we go
back to work. In this case, *less* actually means *more*.

For years, my family has known when I say "My brain is full," I
mean it. I can't decide what to make for dinner, I can't make simple
decisions such as what to wear, nor can I hold a conversation with
any depth. When I hit overload, I can visualize a pot of water boil-
ing over. Anything I try to put in the pot immediately bubbles
right over the top. It's so easy to understand in this analogy that

continuing to add water won't work. If the pot is full, it's full. But when our brains are "full," we still think there's room for more. So we keep adding more work in a desperate cram session.

Human beings are not designed to be constantly "on" while awake. And if you push it to be so, you'll find it has a significant impact—a negative one—on the work you are overfocused on. There was an interesting article written on productivity by Tony Schwartz in the *New York Post*. In a study conducted by Harvard, the biggest predictor of burnout was a lack of two critical elements: sleep and a lack of "do-nothing" time. Keeping your mind in a constant state of focus leads to a saturation point, much like the spinning wheel you see when your computer is loading.

SIGNS YOUR BRAIN NEEDS A BREAK

- You find yourself staring at your computer for hours but not doing the work.
- You spend hours doing simple tasks like answering emails.
- You are in a constant loop of replaying work.
- You feel "brain fog": thoughts aren't "crisp."
- You may have indecision when trying to prioritize tasks.
- You experience numbness or indifference about work quality.
- You aren't as "crisp" or as organized in your conversations.

REBOOTING YOUR BRAIN

If an "easy button" existed, its function would be to reboot your brain. Rewiring thought patterns—not so easy. Changing habits—equally difficult. But preventative maintenance for the brain to keep it fresh isn't as heavy a lift as trying to rewire the whole thing. The goal is simply to place the brain in a position to work its best for us. Here are five things I've found that help your brain the most to avoid a shutdown.

Fifteen-Minute Hard Stop

This is as easy as the old IT "go-to" fix of turning your computer off and then on again. Your brain needs to take a deep breath, something well within your reach. Pivot to a different topic, a different environment, or a different person. Or change all three for at least fifteen minutes. You will find if you do this every time you experience signals that your brain needs a break, the temporary slowing down will more than pay for itself by amping up your productivity on the back end.

The cure for me was spending a few minutes each day visiting with the baby owls in the front yard or giving myself thirty minutes to throw some pottery. I was astounded at how much better I could perform after even a short break. Something about changing the lane I was working in had an immediate healing effect to my brain.

FIFTEEN-MINUTE HARD STOP CHECKLIST

- Walk around the block.
- Listen to your favorite song.
- Call and say "thank you" to someone.

- Buy tickets to a concert you want to see.
- Listen to fifteen minutes of an audio book.
- Do fifteen minutes of meditation.
- Treat yourself to your favorite midday beverage.
- Call a new colleague and ask them about themselves.
- Turn off your computer and sit in silence.
- Visualize your favorite vacation of all time.
- Draw in an adult coloring book.
- Listen to quiet relaxation sounds: nature, rain, thunderstorm, or white noise.

Know When Your Energy Is Highest

Some people do their best thinking first thing in the morning. Some, like myself, need a few hours to rev up the brain; I do my best work from 10:00 a.m. to 1:00 p.m. Other individuals hit their stride the last few hours of the day.

Find the rhythm that works for you and let your brain do the hardest work when you are most productive. I found when I decided to write during the hours my brain worked the best for me, I had less rework and better content. One hour of work produced double the results of what I could produce in the evening. Yet when I sat down to write after dinner, I could all but guarantee that the next day I would realize my work might as well be thrown away! Working at the right time allowed me to work fewer hours and produce more every time.

Early Prioritization

I recommend making big decisions first thing in the morning before you find yourself a victim of run-on Zoom meetings.

Identify the most important decisions to make and tasks to accomplish before you are dead tired. The advice not to make any big decisions until you've "slept on it" is well founded in science. Psychologist and behavioral neuroscientist Daniel Levitin is an expert on work productivity. He describes it like this: "If you spend your day making a bunch of little decisions and it comes time to make a big important one, you're neurologically depleted." Levitin calls this phenomenon "decision fatigue."

The One-Thing Reset

You may get tripped up midday like I do, even after having the best intentions and plans. If you find yourself doing unintentional work—I call it my brain-dead moment—my recommendation is to stop immediately. Write down the one thing you need to be working on right now. The focus of this quick reset has helped me get back on track time after time.

Practice Being Present

One of the downfalls of living in a digital world is our addiction to doing multiple things at once: checking social media while talking to someone or emailing while we are on the phone are only a couple of examples of what we call "multitasking." In reality, we are subconsciously feeding the beast by giving our addicted brains another shot of dopamine. Even if the hit is temporary, it feels so good! If you find it hard to do just one thing at a time, you may be a subconscious adrenaline junkie who keeps giving yourself one more hit for the quick jolt of fresh energy it provides.

But there's a downside to these continual dollops of dopamine: Processing all this information at once creates brain fatigue. I ran across an article about the effect that our fast-paced world is having on people.[3] It struck a chord with me. The author, Johann

Hari, says, "A small study of college students found they only focus on one task for 65 seconds. A different study of office workers found they only focus on average for three minutes. This isn't happening because we all individually became weak-willed. Your focus didn't collapse. It was stolen." With all of the evidence that tells us stress is ruining our brains, it seems to me that we get a positive double whammy when we can unplug from our phones and social media to give our brain back some energy, and "slow the flow" of the constant barrage of information. The quiet spaces these small changes can create are a salve to our overworked brains.

FINAL THOUGHTS

The first step to addressing burnout is to use the same principle that businesses use to become more profitable: they are constantly making decisions about when to give more focus and attention and when to give less of it in order to get the results they need. For you, the equivalent is to look at when and what you will give more of your time to, and when you need to be more efficient with the energy you expend to get your best results. You need to fully understand the levers you can move up and down in order to be your most productive without burning out.

One of the most critical levers requires you to understand how to keep yourself "charged" by creating greater balance. As we discussed in the last chapter, prioritizing your own well-being with the right loyalty mix is the first step to recharging yourself. The second step is working with, instead of against, your brain by listening to the messages it is sending out. While it may seem like a smoke-and-mirrors magic trick, it is true that work output can actually *increase* when you work less.

WALKAWAY ASSIGNMENT

Create your go-to Fifteen-Minute Hard Stop checklist that you can have on hand to use any time you need to unplug. Select from the list in this chapter or create your own list. Write down a list of three to five activities with consideration of each of these categories:

- Physical movement
- Outside time
- Connecting with others
- Senses (hearing, smelling, seeing, tasting, touching)
- Quiet time or meditation
- Hand-eye coordination (such as doing an adult coloring book)
- Setting fun goals (such as planning a trip)

16

Lies About Politics

Lie: Politics is the enemy.

*Truth: Politics is the map for how to get work over
the finish line in a way the company values.*

y job was saved with a napkin conversation over lunch.
I was on the verge of either quitting the company or
getting fired. Quite honestly, it was a race to see which
would happen first. I had never been fired before. It felt strange
not to like my work and to feel like I wasn't succeeding. I realized
this could be the first time in my career that I was not considered
a top performer. I was the one who always excelled. The one who
got fast promotions. The difference-maker. The problem couldn't
be me.

This company was clearly the problem. It was as messed up as
any I had ever seen. Plenty of evidence was available for me to see.
All I had to do was look at the VP of Sales, a maverick who somehow found his way to the top. Unlike me, who had to fight hard
for resources, he had the CEO in his back pocket and constantly

got money to experiment. He had a limited business background and relied on relationships rather than well-researched proposals. It seemed like he had every big proposal or ask already under wraps before it ever came to an executive meeting for discussion, using friendships to get what he wanted.

One of our first interactions gave me my first clue to politics: "I don't need you unless you can help me," he said. Jarring, but it ended up being true. He had brought me into a conversation about changing a commission pay plan for sales. He felt it needed to be adjusted to create greater retention and stop some of the turnover we were getting because too much of the compensation was in a onetime commission. Wanting to do a good job on the project, I immediately dug into the current comp plan. I talked to some salespeople and did some research on different ways we could structure the new plan. I set up meetings with our financial analysts to try modeling a few ideas. Two weeks later, I came armed with ideas and a proposed timeline to roll out whichever plan we selected, but only after we tested and refined it for a quarter to identify any unanticipated problems we needed to fix.

What I didn't realize was that the train had already left the station. When I arrived with compensation plan in hand, I was told he had already decided on the changes and had a phone call with the salespeople. I was furious! It was a haphazard rollout. From my vantage point we were wasting time. We'd have unnecessary rework, because we would not slow down enough to ask the right questions. But that's not how Mr. Maverick saw it. He just looked at me incredulously, as if I was out of touch. Strike one for me.

Then came the napkin incident. Mr. Maverick wandered over to my office at lunch and started drawing another compensation plan idea on a napkin. This new idea would fill a gap and pose minimal cost to the company. Instead of poking holes, I put on my partner hat and started using phrases like, "What if we . . ." instead of "No." We agreed on a solution. It was designed and implemented within two weeks.

It saved my job. Not because I just "rolled over." The truth is that this executive was teaching me (albeit in a blunt way) to pay attention to company politics:

- This company valued speed above all else.
- This company would tolerate mistakes and would trade perfection for quick momentum.
- They tolerated risk well, as long as you could make fast fixes when a correction was needed.
- They wanted to lead rather than lag, which required experimentation and innovation.
- This was a "sink or swim" company, and it required a person to be a doer.

My mistake was not recognizing that company politics—the thing we love to hate—was trying to teach me how to be successful at this company. Mr. Maverick knew this already and had cemented his place in a company that loved his experimental and quick-paced style.

If you are listening to this story and thinking you would have quit the company, I don't fault you for it. To some degree, it's important to feel you are well matched with a company's style of getting things done. But don't be so rigid as to think that you can't survive a company that is different from your natural work style. Sometimes all that is needed is a simple adjustment.

If you are not convinced and still think that company politics is the enemy, you aren't alone.

If you're dissatisfied with your work, company politics makes an easy target. Usually it has a negative connotation. People often complain that it gets in the way of moving their career forward and advantages only a select few—or that it negatively impacts marginalized groups, certain departments, or personalities. Yes, company politics can be maddening. I'm not saying that all politics are good. But the simple and inescapable truth is this: politics exist at every company. People often choose to leave their companies over politics just to find the same thing in a different form at the next company. I'm not suggesting that you should ignore politics. I'm asking you to stare it in the face and realize what it can teach you.

In this chapter, I'll show you why you should stop blaming "brownnosers" who play politics right, and instead look at these important lessons that politics can teach you about your company.

GET TO KNOW YOUR COMPANY'S POLITICS

Paying attention to politics doesn't mean you are going to the dark side. You are simply opening a door to see the landscape better. The greatest advantage to you is that reading the politics of a company doesn't require you to do anything except pay attention to what is going on around you, and this technique is available to every single employee without any cost or requirements. Unlike special skill sets, such as those in the Five Stages of Growth, which take time and testing to begin yielding results, aligning yourself to company politics requires only your observation and action. A watchful eye will allow you to make immediate adjustments.

Learn to value politics as a unique fingerprint
each company has for how to get things done.

You can decide if you dislike a company's politics enough to change companies, but never forget their importance. Stop thinking they hurt you and realize they are teaching you. If you pay attention, they give you the keys to successful company navigation.

I'm embarrassed to admit it took decades for me to realize that politics was my friend. I was able to adjust in each company that employed me, but I was operating in the dark, making changes without a formula and without knowing exactly where to look. If you had asked me then whether paying attention to politics could help my career, I would have told you, "I don't need to stoop that low to get ahead." My view was that politics exposed a rigged system and promoted favoritism—everything that was wrong with companies. When the light finally went on, I was able to make a massive shift that saved me from an embarrassing career failure and a path where I am certain I would have been fired. It would have been an unnecessary stain on my resume because it would have been 100 percent preventable.

I can now see politics in a new light. They are the one area that you can observe and learn from on the first day of your employment and every day thereafter. You can observe the pace and work style that is rewarded and make immediate adjustments without any awkward meetings or performance appraisals. You simply watch and learn how to navigate the waters and win in your organization.

One way you can take stock of where your company falls in terms of politics is to view it as you would a report card. Think about speed, autonomy, line of sight, innovation, and risk. Those are the primary areas where you can see how the company navigates among important stakeholders, including employees. Take a look at what my own politics report card showed me in figure 9. If I were to map the politics from my old company to my new company, they were almost opposite! I nearly learned too late to make the adjustment by applying the politics of my last company to my new one.

Politics Report Card

My Current Company-Tech

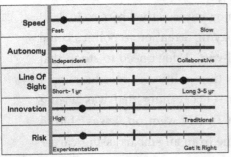

My Old Company-Healthcare

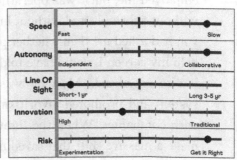

Ahmed Khalid Khan

FIGURE 9

I had blamed brownnosing for this leader's success. I was wrong. What I learned is that he understood the map to the company's culture and that is how he succeeded—not because he was doing anything nefarious. My mistake was still applying my last company's politics to this new company. I had come from a methodical culture where committees had to buy in and make the final decisions, a place where a seamless rollout was a requirement. I almost didn't realize that all I needed to do in order to win was to go faster, even at the cost of a few mistakes.

Each company in which you work will reward work style and pace differently. Don't make the mistake of applying the same style across all companies:

- I would have been fired at the old company for creating a comp plan on a napkin.
- I would have been fired at the new company for taking the time for a thoughtful and seamless rollout.

Yet reversing it and applying the right solution to the right company moved me from laggard to top performer.

What made you a top performer in one company can be the very thing that is your undoing in the next company.

In fly-fishing, the goal is to "match the hatch." A fisherman needs to look at what types of bugs are hatching under or on top of the water to catch a fish. If a certain fly worked last time, it doesn't mean it will work this time. If you don't match the hatch, you may very well come up empty-handed. The same is true with company politics. You've got to match the hatch—know what works in this company environment, not what worked in the last company.

THE FIVE PRINCIPLES OF POLITICS

When you think of politics, there are five specific areas where you will need to pay close attention to read and adjust to your environment (see figure 10).

5 Principles of Politics

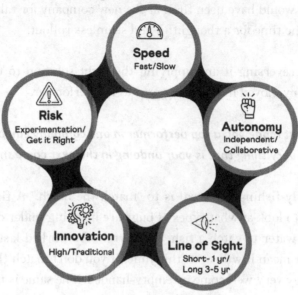

Ahmed Khalid Khan

FIGURE 10

Principle #1: Speed

Some organizations are intentionally methodical, and it serves them well. They want to carefully weigh out the impact of any changes that are introduced to the business. An example would be healthcare giants, such as UnitedHealthcare. They cannot afford haphazard rollouts or mishandled healthcare offerings. Large public companies that are mindful of share price are often in this category, as are industries that are highly regulated.

If you work in one of these organizations, your ideas need to be backed by data, with a strong project plan and multiple levels of buy-in. Any missteps rolling out a new product or program can be detrimental to your career. These companies put pressure on the individual to tie up any loose ends and close any gaps before anything is rolled out. If you are a person who struggles with understanding the downstream dependencies required for a successful implementation, you will need to practice this skill.

More than any other political principle, this one is important to identify early. If you do not understand that your company values speed, and you move too slowly, you'll be identified as someone who can't keep up with the business or a mismatch to the culture. A CFO I worked with used to say this about people who were too slow for the business: "They are all hat and no cattle." In other words, they talk about doing but don't actually get anything done.

Individuals may be top performers in a methodical or thoughtful organization, yet find themselves failing in a fast-moving organization if they cannot make the adjustment. These individuals may make great data-based decisions and execute well-thought-out plans to near perfection. But if the company politics call for speed, you are going to get a label that doesn't feel representative of the good work you are capable of doing. You'll feel rushed, frenetic, anxious, and ill prepared—the opposite of the self-assurance you feel when you know you've done your homework and you are ready for a great rollout.

HELPFUL ADJUSTMENTS

If you need to go faster: In sales, time kills deals, and this is no different. If you spend too much time in preparation, you will be left behind. Focus on the desired outcome being clear, because the tactics to get there will shift. Agree on the next one, two, or three steps to move forward, which is about as far ahead as you can see.

If you need to go slower: The skills you need to employ in a slow environment are project management and strong collaboration. You need a plan where every detail is tied off, and you need to make sure everyone involved has signed off on the project.

Principle #2: Line of Sight

While most companies have some kind of vision of the future, line of sight speaks to how far in advance a company plans and funds the future. Some companies can see three to five years into the future, and they reward solutions that will map to that plan, in steps. For example, a company may believe that the future for partner events is through virtual reality, and they begin funding technology partners to that end.

There is often (but not always) a connection between the size of a company and its line of sight. When a company is mature enough to have processes and roles defined, it likely can look up and out to the future.

On the other end of the spectrum are companies that focus on the *now*. That may seem to be a bad strategy, but it isn't necessarily! Particularly in a disruptive industry (meaning the product or service may completely change the way things are done), speed to gain market share is far more important than thinking about the customer experience five years from now. An example of this would be the residential solar industry ten years ago. At the time, there was no undisputed industry leader, but there were dozens of smaller companies jockeying for position. It was a race for the most panels installed. For many of these companies, the strategy was captured in one word: go! The belief was that whoever installed the most solar panels would be able to own the future of the industry, even if nobody knew then how they could fully benefit from having the most penetration in the market. At one point,

Vivint Solar, where I led HR, was opening an office each week. Chaos? Yes. But it was intentional chaos that ended up paying Blackstone a twenty-seven-fold multiple on its investment when Vivint Solar sold to Sunrun several years later. This would not have been possible without an intense focus on gaining market share as quickly as possible.

HELPFUL ADJUSTMENTS

If you need to adopt a longer line of sight: If this is your company, learning to identify how your project intersects with other departments will be critical. Increasing your cross-department communication to identify potential problems, redundancies, and crossovers where departments are dependent on each other to execute will act like an insurance policy on a successful project.

If you need to adopt a shorter line of sight: If you work in this environment, you don't necessarily know where you'll be several years in the future. So you'll want to implement solutions that can be modified or changed without major disruption. You will want your contracts with vendors or suppliers to be shorter, and to avoid making expensive purchases for systems that require complex implementations. Your best bet is to buy ready-made systems hosted outside the company that allow for some customization.

Principle #3: Autonomy

Some companies allow for a tremendous amount of decision autonomy. Managers can move quickly and independently give the green light for decisions within their sphere. If you've ever been interviewed by a manager who offered you the job at the end of your time block, you know how refreshing it can be.

Small start-ups are often in this category, and it's one of the reasons people like working in these companies. One of the most compelling links to job satisfaction is the ability to make a difference. When a person feels they have some control over decisions, they often also feel they have more control over their destiny in the workplace. Having the freedom to make decisions without unnecessary barriers usually creates incredible work engagement.

On the other end of the spectrum is collaborative decision-making. Some companies like shared mindset around "the way the company does things." This creates an environment where people quickly learn core guiding principles for decisions. As people are included in decisions and discussions, they learn to make proposals and asks that are aligned with the company philosophy. Companies that collaborate as a part of their DNA tend to have panel interviews so they can assess candidates together, and often make decisions through committees where there is an executive sponsor assigned for oversight.

For some, it feels overly bureaucratic and cumbersome to involve so many people in decisions. For others, it provides a greater sense of security: the entire responsibility does not rest with one person alone. While it may feel like collaborative companies are reserved for larger entities, it's not always the case. They can be found at any sized organization and across all industries.

HELPFUL ADJUSTMENTS

If you are in an independent environment: If you aren't used to trusting yourself or your judgment, you can get stuck in analysis paralysis. If the thought of making a mistake stops you from moving forward, make sure you identify a plan B in case your decision doesn't go as planned. Seeing that decisions don't have to be permanent and visualizing alternatives can be powerful in helping you keep momentum.

If you are in a more collaborative environment: If you aren't accustomed to this type of environment, don't make the rookie mistake of surprising a group with your brilliant proposal and have the committee see it the first time collectively. You should never go into a meeting unless you've already had some one-on-one time with key influencers about the direction you are going. It will give you an early preview of objections and allow you to make early adjustments. Involvement equals commitment. Going into any formal ask, you need the greatest influencers on your side.

Principle #4: Innovation

Some industries are marked by their innovation; creativity and fresh ideas are rewarded. Typically, start-ups, particularly those in the tech space, are known for disruptive thinking. Consider Uber, a company that was based on the premise that we should get in a car with complete strangers—exactly what our parents brought us up *not* to do. Or Airbnb, where you wind down a country lane in the middle of nowhere and stay in the home of a complete stranger. Every individual who had a car could be a part-time driver and homeowners could create additional income opportunities by putting out some guest towels and opening their doors. The idea suddenly made sense to us and made side gigs accessible to almost everyone.

Other companies or industries are slower to move and heavily regulated. Taking chances isn't part of their personality. For example, consider the automotive arena. Until Tesla came along, big innovations were few and far between. One car may have a more attractive body, and one may have a more luxurious interior or a more powerful engine. But "innovation" would not be the word I would use to describe the industry. Now there is a self-driving car—an idea that, twenty years ago, I couldn't have imagined would ever be available to everyday consumers. But not every automotive company lacks innovation. Tesla is an example of one that is high on the innovation scale in an industry that has not been known for innovation in a long time.

Is your department or function building or maintaining? The answer will provide a big clue. If it is building, you are likely to see investments in new technology and systems, and the goals are related to creating new services or programs, not just improving the current ones by adding more people.

Watch for how ideas are received. Does the development team have patents? That's a good sign it's on the high end of innovation. Or does the company dip its toe into a new idea but then pull back before it has had time to catch hold? Does it invest only small amounts of money in new ideas?

Note that it isn't necessarily a negative to work in a company that isn't comfortable with a lot of innovation. In such a company, one can excel in their knowledge of the product or service. Instead of going wide (and broadening the products), you can go deep. It also minimizes some of the challenges of making bets on the wrong new ideas. These companies focus on what works—and doing more of it.

The biggest risk? The competition outsmarts you (like Tesla) and changes the game when you are busy doing more of the same.

HELPFUL ADJUSTMENTS

If you are in an innovative environment: Innovation requires more than your own brain coming up with good ideas. If you spend too much time heads-down without looking at what else is happening in the broader business community outside your company, you are starting out behind. Spend at least thirty minutes a day reading business publications so that you are seeing what other thought leaders are talking about, both inside and outside of your industry.

If you are in a traditional environment: You don't have to be boring or accept the status quo to work at a traditional company, but you do need to acknowledge that creative new ideas and approaches are likely better received if they are framed as an "experiment" rather than a permanent solution. Your ability to prove through metrics that the idea worked will help you move it from temporary to permanent.

Principle #5: Risk
Hand in hand with a desire to innovate is a tolerance for risk, even if it means making mistakes. Making changes and taking risks offers the possibility of a big win. These companies make big bets on big ideas. They usually accept a certain amount of failure and aren't as likely to punish individuals when they make a mistake or don't get exactly the desired results. Instead, they use the experience as a learning opportunity to refine and revise the idea for round two, or they move on. This isn't to say that for these companies wasting money is a pastime, because a company's Job #1 is making a profit. The wins must be bigger than the losses. Make a mistake, just don't make the same one again.

It follows, then, that companies that accept high risk may fail at times, requiring layoffs and cuts. But then again, win big, and new hires, new roles, and new departments are created.

Think about WeWork, a company that placed its bets on shared building space for companies and individuals. It had a $47 billion valuation and was the darling of the business world until 2020, when a pandemic sent everyone home. The company's valuation plummeted to $9 billion.[1] Its leadership placed a big bet on a big idea. They just happened to lose . . . at least for now.

But then again, Airbnb is another company with a high tolerance for risk. The business model of using other people's homes to offer alternatives to hotels seemed a little crazy at the time. Airbnb laughed all the way to the bank, growing profits by 280.2 percent in 2021.[2]

HELPFUL ADJUSTMENTS

If you are in a "learn from mistakes" environment: Don't overfocus on selling an idea just because you can convince others it's a good risk to take. Make sure you have thought about the execution and have a strong project management focus. The risks you take still need to be smart risks. Even in a risk-taking company, you can make too many bad bets.

If you are in a "make no mistakes" environment: If project management is not a strength, you will benefit from learning basic methodologies and using project management software to keep everyone on track. There is too much at stake to risk a failure due to poor planning. My experience is that without a good project manager, even the best projects fail. It's a good skill to have regardless of the company politics. But if mistakes are penalized, it's an even better idea.

FINAL THOUGHTS

Reframe your thinking from believing that politics is a game you play. Politics in its purest form is not gamesmanship. Of all the principles I teach, this is the one that people tend to have the most difficulty reframing positively. But the power in rethinking politics will be infinitely impactful on your career. A company's politics can show you how to navigate the company.

WALKAWAY ASSIGNMENT

Identify someone in your company who consistently gets ahead. Challenge yourself to set aside your preconceived ideas of how or why this person is successful and ask yourself these questions:

1. What would their Politics Graph look like? How are they using politics to get work across the finish line?
2. What does my Politics Graph look like? What adjustments do I need to make?

Politics Report Card

My Company Politics

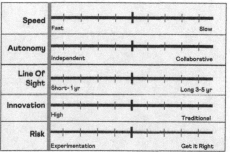

My Work Style

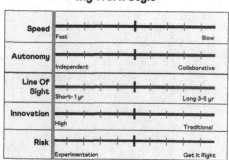

Ahmed Khalid Khan

CONCLUSION

Should I Stay or Should I Go?

Lie: Leaving to start a new job will eliminate my burnout and solve my work problems.

Truth: Running too fast from a job you hate without understanding why it isn't working for you will land you in another bad job.

I was three children into my first marriage when I learned my husband was having an affair with another man. While I'm pretty sure I should have known all along, the fact remains that I did not. When I began dating again, it was tempting to run into the arms of the first man who would take me. I just wanted to be loved for who I was—all of me.

That may seem like a strange and personal example to hear in a book about the workplace. But leaving jobs and leaving relationships have a few similarities: If we aren't careful, we may leap from a bad one directly into another bad one. After all, when everything

286 THE UNSPOKEN TRUTHS FOR CAREER SUCCESS

seems broken in the work relationship we are in, the other options look so good! Where jobs are concerned, it can be tempting to run from one that feels miserable. But running from a bad job isn't going to end well for you until you know why it didn't work and what you need in the next role. Just like relationships.

I get to visit every day with individuals who are making big career decisions. Most clients lead with this line: *I just can't stand it anymore.*

What I have learned in my work with clients is that the "it" they can't stand anymore needs to be identified before they can make a good decision about whether to stay or go. People often decide to go without truly understanding why the job isn't working for them and whether they can fix what is broken and stay. When individuals feel dissatisfied at work, they may find it hard to see any other option besides *I've got to get out of here.*

My job is to slow people and their decision-making down before they make the leap. There are far more options than they realize and a host of considerations to make before exiting becomes their plan of choice. Even if an exit is the right decision, a thoughtful one can make all the difference.

If you are leaving your company because you believe starting over will solve everything, know that it's a crapshoot at best.

This chapter isn't going to provide the easy answer you may have hoped for. Whether to stay or go is a deeply personal decision that nobody can make for you. People leave or stay for hundreds of different reasons. However, regardless of your decision, there is a strategic way to go about it. These are the goals I have for you:

- If you leave, plan your exit strategically so you have leverage to get the best next job.
- If you stay, make sure you have a plan to create a fresh 2.0 version of your career.
- If you start over, be clear on the gives and takes that come with the new chapter.
- If you leave the workforce altogether, time it wisely to benefit your bank account.

I want your decision to be a deliberate one and your next step in your career journey to be one that brings you closer to the satisfaction you are seeking.

In this chapter, I will take you through a framework that will help you understand the deeper *why* that is driving your desire to leave. This methodology will help you determine a course of action that will give you a better outcome than just guessing. Whichever path you choose, there are steps you need to understand to move you into your next chapter successfully.

IT MAY NOT BE THE JOB

I want every single person thinking of leaving to make an honest assessment: Is it the job or the difficult conditions of our current world that has you wanting to leave? We are living in a time when it is hard to be a human. I don't say this to rub it in. But I want you to factor it in to any decision to leave your company. Consider that almost 80 percent of people surveyed are just plain angry right now. Chris Cillizza, CNN editor-at-large, wrote an article called "We're All Just So Damn Angry."[1] He put voice to something that resonates: There is a collective frustration with the way things are going in the world regardless of political affiliation.

We are all a bit tired, frustrated, and seeking peace. It may be possible that your frustration at work is colored by what is happening in the world at large.

Your work burnout may be in part a result of life burnout.
If that's the case, moving to a new job won't fix the problem.
It's just going to change the physical location where
you are feeling frustration each day.

When life is heavy all around, everything feels hard. Separating the job from how life feels overall is not easy, but it needs to be part of your assessment. Part of the answer may be to look at what's going on in the world around you and how much extra baggage you're carrying. Couple that with all that you are carrying at work, and you have a lot to think about.

THE FIVE CHOICES

People often think they have only two choices: to stay or to go. But there are five basic choices to consider, each with a different set of pros and cons. Let's take a look at each one.

Stay and Do Nothing Different

It sounds like a defeatist view to stay when you aren't happy. But this could be an entirely reasonable choice if your life outside of work is complex, if you have significant equity vesting soon, or you decide that there are some compensatory benefits that are valuable to you (such as a flexible work environment). Sometimes continuing exactly what we are doing without making a lot of changes is the right answer and it can lead to many additional years at a job.

PROS

✓ You are a proven entity already.

✓ No extra energy expenditure.

✓ Shows stability on a resume.

CONS

✗ Staying means more of the same dissatisfaction.

✗ Long-term burnout has health impacts.

✗ Unhappiness spills over into other parts of life.

Stay and Reinvent Your Career

Pushing the reset button at your current job—treating it like a new job without actually changing jobs—can help an individual work their way out of a slump with a fraction of the effort of getting a new job. Staying at your job, particularly when you are not experiencing satisfaction day to day, may seem like a decision to stay miserable. But reinventing the 2.0 version of yourself can be done with great success. I've done it and I've seen many others do it.

PROS

✓ You have the inside track on best departments and roles.

✓ Vesting of 401(k) and/or equity isn't lost.

✓ Showing in-company advancement looks great on your resume.

CONS

✗ If you are overcoming a negative perception of you, it will take some effort.

✗ It's easy to fall back into old patterns, and change requires discipline.

✗ You are jaded from your current experience.

New Company and Same Career Track

Searching for and securing a new job can be a tremendous boost to one's self-esteem. Being "picked" as the one a company chooses to hire is often the jump-start a person needs to reenergize themselves. Like a new relationship, it shows all the promise without any of the baggage of one's last workplace.

PROS

✓ You get to walk away from the problems of your company and make a fresh start.

✓ It's a fast way to level up in your title, pay, and role.

✓ You can choose a company whose politics suit your natural style.

CONS

✗ You will have to start over, proving yourself to a company.

✗ You are taking a risk as to whether the new company is all it claims to be.

✗ You are beginning all over again creating work social circles.

New Company and Complete Career Pivot

It's not easy to leave one's career and start on an entirely new track. But I've watched hundreds of people do it. After the initial shock wears off—usually in about six months—those who make deliberate pivots usually love the outcome. But the decision to pivot needs to be deliberate, because it often comes with an initial pay cut. If someone chooses wisely, however, they can make up for the initial loss and quickly create career momentum.

PROS

  ✓ After the initial adjustment, individuals often report feeling "alive" again.

  ✓ It opens up infinite new possibilities and new career tracks.

  ✓ You know yourself (and where you excel) better after some career trial and error.

CONS

  ✗ You will take a pay cut for a period of time.

  ✗ There will be additional training and effort required to catch up.

  ✗ It's scary, really scary.

Become a Gig Worker or Contractor

This used to be the option more often for those who couldn't find full-time employment or those who wanted some control of their work schedule. But gig work has gone mainstream, and I predict it will become the option of choice over the next decade. It offers great earning potential, tax deductions, and all the flexibility today's worker wants.

PROS

  ✓ Work can ramp up or down based on individual need.

  ✓ Can offer the most control over one's pay—you want more, you work more.

  ✓ You are not permanently connected to a company you may not like.

CONS

  ✗ You can't just show up every day for a paycheck; you have to seek new business.

✗ You pay for your benefits and don't get paid time off.

✗ There is additional stress in running your own business—taxes, contracts, billing, and so on.

FINAL CONSIDERATIONS BEFORE YOU LEAVE

Any decision—whether you stay, leave immediately, or plan a future leave—should be deliberate. Similar to a hasty exit from a marriage, you are bound to make mistakes if, in your desire to eliminate the pain, you quickly jump out of your situation. I have seen many people leave their intolerable jobs in a hurry only to land at another intolerable job and then have to make the difficult decision whether to completely blow up their resume and leave again or stick it out in an equally miserable situation to preserve their resume. You will find there is a direct correlation between speed and the outcome of your next opportunity.

When it comes to deciding to stay or to go,
speed is the enemy.

Slow roll the change. Job or career changes should be thoughtful. Strategic. Measured. You'd better be clear about what you want in the next company. Even if moving is the right decision, a thoughtful approach to the transition can create more leverage for better pay and a better pick.

There is an energy equation to consider before changing jobs. Make no mistake: searching for a job requires extra energy. And proving yourself all over again in a new company is another six to twelve months of extra energy expended. I am not suggesting you need to stay because it's too much work to change jobs. You need to change jobs when it makes sense for you. Before you decide the answer is to leave your job, consider the energy you expend seeking a new job—brushing up your resume and interview skills, fine-tuning your network of connections, and scanning job descriptions, not to mention the pressure to perform in your interview. Once you are there, you will need to start over on developing your internal networks, learning how the company operates and what they value, and getting some early wins that require serious up-front effort.

Going into a new job search with a realistic expectation you'll need to give an extra 20 percent over the next year.

It's also easy to forget that as humans we hate discomfort. It's the root of our avoidance of conflict, but it's also the root of any big life decision, including changing jobs. Sometimes we make a change only when the discomfort of staying seems worse than the discomfort of leaving.

Once you've determined you aren't happy in your job, you don't escape the discomfort with a new job. You've just signed up for delayed discomfort as you start to prove your worth to a new employer all over again.

It's a lot to take in. It's a weighty decision, but the final answer is up to you. Think about all the lies we've busted in this book, and all the truths that exist in your company. The knowledge that you have about the realities of your workplace can help guide you. You may think the decision is the endpoint, but it is just the beginning. Now you need a strategy to leave or stay in a way that is most beneficial to your future. Here are a few questions to ask before you make any major moves:

- If you are expending 20 percent extra energy to make the move and then prove yourself, how could you have spent that same energy to change your current workplace experience?
- If you are feeling burned out already, do you have that extra 20 percent to give?
- Will a new job fix what's broken, or is the real problem something in your personal life that needs to get addressed? If you weigh this into the equation, it's possible that staying—with some modifications—may be a good answer for you.
- If you are going to leave, do you have a good understanding of your values rankings and the type of opportunity that is likely to be a match for you?
- Which kind of discomfort do you want to sign up for? Discomfort of proving yourself in a new role or the discomfort of reinventing yourself at your current company?

Many people aren't sure which of these five paths to pursue, so they simply take the path of least resistance. This strategy often does not end well. If you want to make a solid choice, you need to know what you value in the workplace and what is currently missing.

The good news is you have some tools to help you make your decision.

USE A VALUES ANALYSIS
TO DETERMINE YOUR NEXT MOVE

Before you leave, it's critical to understand what your current company is not providing for you, as well as the most valued factors to look for in the next company. Many of my clients have a vague idea of why they are no longer happy at work, but when I ask them to identify what they want to look for in a new company, it is difficult for them to be specific. What I hear most often is that they want to find a company that "values its people," a catchall for about every problem that contributes to disengagement.

Rather than broad statements, an effective approach is to drill into the real reasons an individual is experiencing a disconnect with their company. It's rarely the reason they think it is. A values analysis helps you better understand your own work personality profile and identify with greater specificity what you need and value in a work experience. It shows where the gaps are with your current company. The result can help you make a better choice when you make a change.

If the reason for wanting to leave your company is overly broad—such as being overworked, underpaid, or underappreciated—I challenge you to examine one level deeper. You'll find that it's incredibly difficult to assess how a potential new company would stack up. In generalizing your reasons to leave, you miss the opportunity to understand what's really going on with your work experience. Seeing the analysis in front of you can help you determine if it's a fixable problem or if it's time to move on.

You need to understand the unique formula for the environment where you will thrive. A job where much of the work is defined well and processes run smoothly is a dream for one person, but a boring choice for another. Likewise, for the right individual it's like pure oxygen to be given freedom to experiment and build without the constraints of predefined processes.

In my own journey, the story I was telling myself was that I was "tired" and didn't feel "alive" any longer. After this exercise, I was stunned to see why I wasn't satisfied in my job any longer. After seeing the results of this analysis, I realized that these vague descriptors were masking the real problem: I had grown into a mismatch with my company. I had come in and built the infrastructure from scratch and now that it was working, I wasn't as energized. We were in maintenance mode. I could see that the company was no longer stretching me. I wasn't learning and growing at a pace that aligned with my work values.

Now, instead of leaving to find a company where I could feel "alive," I understood the conditions that would create that experience for me. I was a better fit for a fast-growing company or an entrepreneurial venture where I could try new ideas. Let me show you my own chart so you can see how I arrived at this conclusion:

I highlighted the two areas where there was a value ranking differential greater than two points: learning/growth and autonomy.

What My Own Results Suggest

- **Learning:** I have to be learning and growing in a job. My current job was no longer providing this for me, although it had for several years. I'm a builder. Once the company is running smoothly, I lose interest because that need is no longer being met.
- **Security:** I could pursue entrepreneurial ventures because security wasn't a high value for me. I was financially secure and I could look at start-ups or otherwise risky ventures like self-employment.

Work Values Rankings

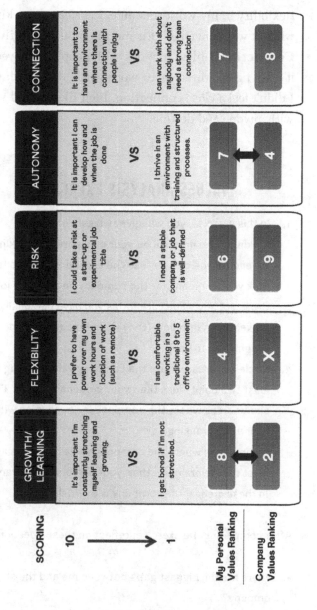

SCORING	GROWTH/ LEARNING	FLEXIBILITY	RISK	AUTONOMY	CONNECTION
10 → 1	It's important I'm constantly stretching myself learning and growing. VS I get bored if I'm not stretched.	I prefer to have power over my own work hours and location of work (such as remote) VS I am comfortable working in a traditional 9 to 5 office environment	I could take a risk at a start-up or experimental job title VS I need a stable company or job that is well-defined	It is important I can develop how and when the job is done VS I thrive in an environment with training and structured processes.	It is important to have an environment where there is connection with people I enjoy VS I can work with about anybody and don't need a strong team connection
My Personal Values Ranking	8	4	6	7	7
Company Values Ranking	2	X	9	4	8

Ahmed Khalid Khan

- **Autonomy:** As I became an empty nester, I craved more flexibility in my work schedule. I preferred working when it was convenient for me, and not nine to five.
- **Connection:** I liked to work with people I enjoyed, but it wasn't a deal breaker to work with others with whom I didn't feel a close connection. I felt like I could work with anyone and do fine.

VALUES ANALYSIS EXERCISE

1. In this exercise, you will give two sets of 1 to 10 rankings. The first will be your own personal rankings for each of the categories. The second set will be to rank your company (or the company you want to join).

2. Cross out any value categories you have personally ranked at a 5 or below (they do not meet a threshold of a high value to you).

3. Circle any areas where the company value ranking is at least two points less than your personal ranking. This shows areas where the company is not aligning with your values ranking.

4. Ignore areas where the company value ranking is at least two points more than your personal value ranking. In these arenas, the company is overdelivering.

After completing the exercise, reflect on these questions:

- Where are the biggest gaps between me and the company?
- What does this tell me about what I need?

- Can I see a path in my current company to close the gaps?
- If I cannot see a path to stay, what do the scoring gaps between me and my company suggest I need to look for?

Now that you have seen how the values analysis works and you have clarity about what is missing in your current workplace situation, let's explore the choices you have in front of you and the accompanying pros and cons.

MY OWN DECISION TO PIVOT CAREERS

I don't want to publish this story for obvious reasons. It's bad enough to admit my husband was right privately, let alone publicly. But his wisdom is what got me to this place, writing this book. I will forever be grateful for his truth-telling.

My husband laid it out in the most honest but infuriating way: "I'm just not sure I like the person you are becoming. You've either got to leave or find a way to find yourself again. Because this is not healthy. For you, or for us."

And there it was. The truth laid out in an indisputable way.

The argument started when my husband asked why I didn't respond to a text at 8:00 p.m. asking if he should wait until I got home to have dinner together. Instead of the five seconds it would have taken to respond properly to his kind request, I instead pushed the quick auto-respond button: "Can I call you later?"

In my mind, this was a quick way to say to him, "I'm here. I see you are trying to reach me. Can't talk." I saw it as efficient. I had forgotten that even our small connection moments had value.

My Personal Rankings

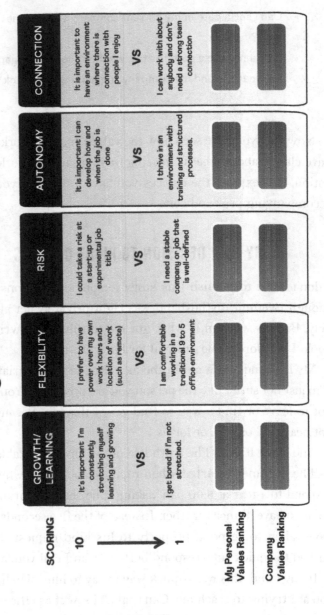

	GROWTH/ LEARNING	FLEXIBILITY	RISK	AUTONOMY	CONNECTION
	It's important I'm constantly stretching myself learning and growing	I prefer to have power over my own work hours and location of work (such as remote)	I could take a risk at a start-up or experimental job title	It is important I can develop how and when the job is done	It is important to have an environment where there is connection with people I enjoy
	VS	VS	VS	VS	VS
	I get bored if I'm not stretched.	I am comfortable working in a traditional 9 to 5 office environment	I need a stable company or job that is well-defined	I thrive in an environment with training and structured processes.	I can work with about anybody and don't need a strong team connection

SCORING 10 → 1

My Personal Values Ranking

Company Values Ranking

Ahmed Khalid Khan

At home later that evening our conversation escalated quickly. "Do you think I'm lying about work? Do you think I *like* this?" As the familiar argument picked up steam, I tried to explain the pressures of work. I wanted to come home earlier, but it would mean falling further behind. "After all," I said, "I only need to be here a few more years to get my options vested and then I can get back to normal."

That weekend became one of deep reflection about how I had gotten to this place again and what I was going to do about it. I had little to give at the end of the day. I was on autopilot and had determined I had to accept this hollow life. Too much money and too many stock options at play. I told myself I needed to make sacrifices now so that later we would have the full freedom we wanted. Then, I thought, I could magically transform back into the fun person I used to be.

This conversation was the final tipping point for a personal decision to leave behind the corporate world forever.

What may surprise you is that I didn't leave because of the hours. I thought deeply about whether the problem was me or the job (the answer was both). I did a values analysis (because who doesn't love a good numbers-based analysis) and I was able to identify what was really missing for me in the job and what I needed.

I knew I wanted to work. I love it and it fills me up. I knew I wanted to take a risk and a challenge without the constraints of the corporate environment. I was able to make a thoughtful and deliberate exit, which helped me with my final pivot to become the Job Doctor.

I am so glad I stayed the additional year because it allowed me to practice all that I try to teach my clients about the power to reframe and create a better experience. I loved my remaining time at the company. I was able to finish some important legacy projects. I left feeling good about my ending. Had I left in the heat of the moment, I would have had temporary relief, but I would not have ended on the high point I wanted for myself after a twenty-five-year career in corporate America.

THE NEXT STEP IN YOUR JOURNEY

In my own career, I've made all five of the decision options, including creating a new version of me within the company where I thought I would never find satisfaction. However, more compelling are the examples of clients, old and young, from truck drivers to software developers to CEOs, who have also made their own decisions and found great happiness at work again. Let them motivate you to know you can have a good ending to your story as well:

- Nessa quit her job as a hospitality worker after a divorce and decided she wanted to improve her future life. She found a school that helps women take a twelve-weekend training program to help them land tech jobs. A few years after completing the program and working her way up, she has gone from $24,000 a year to over $100,000.
- Jessica loved what her job was supposed to be but was disillusioned by a reality that didn't match. The company wasn't getting the performance it expected out of the new franchise managers. Instead of watching the results continue to decline, she chose to reframe her thinking. Instead of believing she was not allowed to be strategic, she mustered the courage to speak to the CEO

honestly about how the company could turn around and how she could play a part. After all, she had nothing to lose if the alternative was leaving. The conversation not only didn't get her fired, but it helped her walk away with new confidence and the budget to try an innovative training approach to onboard and train new franchise leaders.

- Robin chose to leave the company before they were fired. Upon understanding the mismatch to their values rankings, Robin decided to reenter the corporate world, but this time in a small start-up. Instead of a niche role, which felt one-dimensional and boring, a smaller company offered variability and a broader job description. Three years and three promotions later, they are the head of operations at a fast-growing company where they manage more than one hundred people.

- Ben left his entire career behind as a teacher to work in sales at Uber Eats. Several promotions later he is convinced he's stumbled into his passion, realizing making an impact was his primary driver and he could better see the immediate impacts in an industry that moved faster and allowed for greater risk-taking.

These are examples of individuals who regained control of their voice and their career by daring to get uncomfortable and by recognizing they have a voice and a choice in everything that happens in the workforce. They let go of the lies and harnessed the power of the truths in their own companies and lives.

TRUTHS OF THE WORKFORCE

- Companies will take as much as you will give.
- A company isn't good or bad; it is simply aligned for results.
- You don't have an accurate view of how others perceive you.
- Conflict doesn't damage your career but a lack of it will.
- Your manager's perception of you is reality.
- The skill that got you here isn't the skill that will get you to the next level.
- Following your job description won't earn you the promotion.
- You're only as relevant as your last accomplishment.
- Working hard doesn't mean you are adding value.
- Knowledge is power.
- Money goes to those who ask, not to those who wait.
- Your results are your greatest leverage.
- Never be more loyal to a company than it can be to you.
- Work-life balance is your job and not your manager's.
- Politics isn't the enemy.

Where will you be a year from now? Will you have a similar story to tell?

My deepest wish as the Job Doctor is that you find the courage to look deeply, make an honest assessment, and take the leap to create a better workplace experience and a better future. Be deliberate. Be brave.

You've got this.

ENDNOTES

CHAPTER 1

1. Ashley Abramson, "Burnout and Stress Are Everywhere," *Monitor on Psychology* 53, no. 1 (January 1, 2022): 72, https://www.apa.org/monitor /2022/01/special-burnout-stress.
2. Jena McGregor, "Careers Weekly: All the Other Names for the 'Great Resignation,' Omicron Is Crashing Return to Office Plans and More," *Forbes*, December 14, 2021, https://www.apa.org/monitor/2022/01 /special-burnout-stress.

CHAPTER 3

1. Ethan Burris, Elizabeth McCune, and Dawn Klinghoffer, "When Employees Speak Up, Companies Win." *MIT Sloan Management Review*, November 17, 2020, https://sloanreview.mit.edu/article/when-employees -speak-up-companies-win/.

CHAPTER 7

1. The 2019 Employee Engagement and Modern Workplace Report, Bonusly Research, Boulder, Colorado, https://go.bonus.ly/2019-employee -engagement-and-modern-workplace-report.

CHAPTER 10

1. Tony Schwartz, "The Power of Starting with 'Yes,'" *New York Times*, April 17, 2015, https://www.nytimes.com/2015/04/18/business/dealbook /the-power-of-starting-with-yes.html.

2. Kyle Benson, "The Magic Relationship Ratio, According to Science," The Gottman Institute, https://www.gottman.com/blog/the-magic-relationship-ratio-according-science/.

CHAPTER 11

1. Adam Bryant and Kevin Sharer, "Are You Really Listening?" *Harvard Business Review*, March–April 2021, https://hbr.org/2021/03/are-you-really-listening.

CHAPTER 12

1. Ben LeFort, "How to Manage Money as a Young Professional," Making of a Millionaire, August 13, 2020, https://www.benlefort.com/post/how-to-manage-money-as-a-young-professional. Charts courtesy of Steve Littlefield.

CHAPTER 13

1. Krithika Varagur, "When Should You Think Twice About Salary Negotiation?" *Wall Street Journal*, February 28, 2021, https://www.wsj.com/articles/when-should-you-think-twice-about-salary-negotiation-11614513601.
2. Tanya Tarr, "How Much Is Too Much When You're Negotiating a Raise?" Fairygodboss, n.d., https://fairygodboss.com/articles/how-much-is-too-much-when-you-re-negotiating-a-raise#.

CHAPTER 14

1. Shruti Bhargava, Bo Finneman, Jennifer Schmidt, and Emma Spagnuolo, "The Young and the Restless: Generation Z in America," McKinsey & Company, March 20, 2020, https://www.mckinsey.com/industries/retail/our-insights/the-young-and-the-restless-generation-z-in-america.

CHAPTER 15

1. Jake Rossen, "This Is Your Brain on Drugs: Any Questions About the Most Famous Anti-Drug Ad?" Mental Floss, May 18, 2017, https://www.mentalfloss.com/article/500800/most-famous-anti-drug-ad-turns-30-any-questions.

2. Society of Human Resources Management, "The Problem with Burnout," August 2017, https://www.shrm.org/hr-today/news/hr-magazine /0817/pages/infographic-the-problem-with-burnout.aspx.
3. Johann Hari, "Your Attention Didn't Collapse. It Was Stolen," *Guardian*, January 2, 2022, https://www.theguardian.com/science/2022/jan/02 /attention-span-focus-screens-apps-smartphones-social-media.

CHAPTER 16

1. Samantha Subin, "Ousted WeWork CEO Says $47 Billion Valuation Went to His Head before Botched IPO," CNBC, November 9, 2021, https://www.cnbc.com/2021/11/09/ousted-wework-ceo-adam-neumann -47-billion-valuation-went-to-his-head.html.
2. Airbnb Statistics (2022): User & Market Growth Data, iProperty Management, May 4, 2022, https://ipropertymanagement.com/research /airbnb-statistics.

CONCLUSION

1. Chris Cillizza, "We're All Just So Damn Angry," CNN.com, September 10, 2021, https://www.cnn.com/2021/09/10/politics/anger-american -electorate-cnn-poll/index.html.

INDEX

A

achievers (Stage 2), 161–165
Airbnb, 279
alignment, 23, 170–171, 172, 183–184
analysis paralysis, 278
"Are You Really Listening?" (Bryant
and Sharer), 188
autonomy, politics of, 277–279
autonomy values, 297–298, 300

B

beliefs, revising. *See* reframing
big-ask bucket, 246–247
bonuses, 225, 226
brain reboot, 262–265
brains and burnout, 258–261
Bryant, Adam, 188
buckets for work-life balance, 244–
    247
budget angle, 33
budgets
    changes to, 27
    managers and, 29–30
    resources, battle for, 184–185
builders (Stage 4), 181–185
burnout. *See also* exits; loyalty and
        work-life balance
    about, 14, 253–255

brain and, 258–261
brain reboot, 262–265
control and, 4–5
as growing problem, 4–6
life burnout, 288
MBI definition of, 4
productivity myths, 255–258
buy-in, securing, 181

C

candidate gap, 100
career pivots, 290–291
cell phone stipends, 227
change, constant, 157
"Choices" discussion, the, 247–250
Cillizza, Chris, 287
collaborative decision making,
        politics of, 278
collaborators (Stage 3), 170–177
communication and speaking up. *See
        also* conflict
    GAP model for, 133–138
    halfway conversations, 46–49, 61
    job satisfaction and, 43–46
    with managers in Stage 1 vs. Stage
        2, 163–164
    performance clues, paying
        attention to, 65–69

communication and speaking up
  (*cont.*)
 risk avoidance, 41–43
 you are part of the problem, 40–41
companies
 aligning with, 23, 170–171, 183–184
 dueling visions and the gap in,
  86–88
 employees, HR, and managers, 24
 governing principles of, 37–38
 HR, problem with, 33–37
 managers, problem with, 29–33
 predictability of, 20–22
 profit and revenue as priority, 22,
  24–29, 229
complaint/concern angle, 37
conflict
 about, 121–125
 avoidance of, 40, 42, 171
 case study, 132–133
 "do this and not that," 138–140
 GAP model for communication,
  133–138, 141
 good conflict, striving for, 126–128
 good intent, assuming, 128–131,
  141–142
 ground rules for candid
  conversations, 125–126
 partnerships and, 172–173
 Stage 4 and, 181–182
 three magic phrases, 131
connection values, 297–298, 300
consistency, 157–160
contract gap, 100–101
contractors, 172, 291–292
control, sense of, 4–5, 42–43
Corel Corporation, 176–177
Covey, Stephen R., 1, 90, 125, 134,
  240
Covey Leadership Center, 90–91, 121

critical thinking skills, 161–162
critical work, identifying, 242–243
cross-functional projects
 feedback and, 79
 funding, 172
 learning to manage, 150
 partnerships, 171–177
 Stage 5 and, 169, 191–192
 talent management and, 73
culture, organizational. *See* politics
curiosity, 104–105
customer advocacy, data and, 113
customer gap, 100

D
dark data, 110
dashboards, 116
data
 case study, 111–112
 dark, 110
 metrics, 114–115
 in pay negotiations, 223
 as power, 109–112
 practical uses of, 112–114
 Stage 3 and, 170
deadlines, 157
decision fatigue, 263–264
development plans, 71–76
directors and vice presidents/the
  builders (Stage 4), 181–185
disobedience, intelligent, 158
doers (Stage 1), 156–161
dopamine, 264
"do this, not that" communication,
  138–140

E
early-stage careers
 about, 9
 gap case study, 90–91

manager, relationship with, 163–164

skill deficiencies in, 148–149

Stage 1 (entry level/the doers), 156–161

Stage 2 (supervisors and individual contributors/the achievers), 161–165

education gap, 100

energy equation, 292–294

entry level/the doers (Stage 1), 156–161

equity, 226

executives. *See* senior careers

exits. *See also* firings and layoffs

  about, 285–287

  burnout and changing jobs, 256–257

  energy equation, 292–294

  examples of choices, 299–303

  five basic choices, 288–292

  halfway conversations and, 48

  the job vs. world conditions, 287–288

  leverage and negotiation, 217–219

  prenegotiated severance, 226

  severance, negotiated, 35, 36, 212, 219, 226

  severance case study, 176–177

  slow and deliberate, 292

  values analysis, 295–301

expanders (Stage 5), 185–193

experiences and exposures, in development plans, 72–74

experiment angle, 32

experimentation, 162, 165

F

feedback. *See also* performance

  360-degree, 78–79

clues, 60

communication clues, 65–69

data and, 113

Feedback Four-Pack, 79–81

quick validates, 77–78

self-directed, 76–81

taking seriously, 59

feelings vs. results, 27–28

fifteen-minute hard stop, 262–263

firings and layoffs. *See also* exits

  fear of speaking up and, 43–44

  loyalty and, 229–230, 237–238

  not seeing it coming, 57–58, 65–66

  process not followed in, 36

Five Stages of Growth Model

  about, 155–156

  line of sight by stage, 192

  Stage 1 (entry level/the doers), 156–161

  Stage 2 (supervisors and individual contributors/the achievers), 161–165

  Stage 3 (mid-level professionals/ the collaborators), 170–177

  Stage 4 (directors and vice presidents/the builders), 181–185

  Stage 5 (senior vice presidents and C-suite/the expanders), 185–193

flexibility values, 297, 300

flexible work schedules, 224

G

gaps

  about, 86–88

  candidate gap, 100

  case studies, 90–95

  conflict, GAP model for, 133–138, 141

  contract gap, 100–101

gaps (*cont.*)
  customer gap, 100
  education gap, 100
  Gap Worksheet, 96–99
  good-to-great/access/plan (GAP), 95–96
  information gap, 99
  innovations gap, 101
  job descriptions vs. hard workers and, 83–86
  loyalty gap, 233–236
  maintenance work and, 101–102
  perks gap, 100
  picking gaps, 88–90, 95–96
  speed gap, 100
  values analysis and, 295, 298–299
  "what we didn't know" gap, 101
Gen Z, 232
get-input bucket, 245–246
gig work, 291–292
Godin, Seth, 84
good intent, assuming, 128–131, 141–142
Gottman, John, 174
Great Resignation, 5, 41
Grenny, Joseph, 134
growth/learning values, 296–297, 300

H
halfway conversations, 46–49, 61
hard stop, fifteen-minute, 262–263
hard workers, 84–85. *See also* burnout; loyalty and work-life balance
Hari, Johann, 264–265
home office, negotiation for, 226
humane leadership, 186
human resources (HR)
  angles to use with, 36–37

partnerships and, 175
risk as priority of, 33–37
what to expect from, 35

I
if-then proposals, 223–224
information gap, 99
information gathering, 115–118. *See also* data
innovation, politics of, 279–281
innovations gap, 101
Interact Performance Systems, 134
interdependence, 167, 170–171

J
job descriptions vs. adding value, 83–84, 88–89
Jobs, Steve, 165
job satisfaction
  autonomy and, 278
  doing the right work and, 239
  loyalty and, 231
  reclaiming, 5, 7, 50, 250
  speaking up and, 43–46
just-do-it bucket, 244–245

K
knowledge as power, 103

L
layoffs. *See* firings and layoffs
learning values, 296–297, 300
leaving a job. *See* exits
LeFort, Ben, 197–198
legal departments and partnerships, 175
level-up angle, 33
leverage
  about, 209–212
  case studies, 216, 217–219

in exiting, 217–219
in pay negotiations, 213–217, 222
positive and negative, 212–213
situational, 215
lies
about burnout, 253
about communication, 39–41
about companies, 19
about conflict, 121, 125
about interdependence, 167
about leaving a job, 285
about leverage, 209
about loyalty, 229, 232
about pay, 195
about performance, 57–59
about politics, 267
about power, 103–106, 118
about promotability, 143, 155
about speed, 179
about working hard, 83–86
of the workforce, 10–14
line of sight, 192, 276–277
listening ecosystem, 186, 188–190
loyalty and work-life balance. *See also*
    burnout
about, 13, 229–232
balance buckets, 244–247
the "Choices" discussion, 247–250
fear of being fired, 237–238
the loyalty equation, 232–233
the loyalty gap, 233–236
proving yourself, 238–239
the 10 percent miracle, 239–243
your responsibility, 236–237

M
maintenance work, streamlining,
    101–102
managers
angles to use with, 32–33

behavior toward you, 61–65
budget goals and, 29–30, 31
communication clues from, 65–69
complaints about, 29, 30–31
data used with, 31
get-input balance bucket and,
    245–246
halfway conversations and, 47–48,
    61
people-management skills and, 30,
    31–32
questions for, 159
in Stage 1 vs. Stage 2, 163–164
what to expect from, 31–32
managing up, 157–158, 170
marketing, 114, 175
Maslach, Christina, 4
Maslach Burnout Inventory (MBI), 4
McCune, Elizabeth, 44
McMillan, Ron, 134
meetings
being on time, 157
canceled, 63
email follow-ups, 62
halfway conversations in, 47–48
mentoring, 74–75
metrics, 114–115
micromanaging, 11, 30, 62, 79, 168
middle-stage careers
about, 9
gap case study, 91–93
skill deficiencies in, 148–149
Stage 3 (mid-level professionals/
    the collaborators), 170–177
mid-level professionals/the
    collaborators (Stage 3),
    170–177
mind maps, 119
mistakes, 158, 165
"multitasking," 264

N

negotiation. *See* leverage; pay and pay raises
news, current, 116, 117–118
"no's," limiting, 174–177

O

on time, being, 157
outside experts, 172
outside opinions, 172
outsourcing, 172
overachievers and promotability, 150

P

partnerships
  limiting "no's" in, 174–177
  Stage 3, teams, and, 171–173
Patterson, Kerry, 134
pay and pay raises
  about, 13, 195–197
  during annual review cycle vs. outside the cycle, 204–206
  bonuses, 225, 226
  compounding returns, 197–198
  cost of waiting, 198–201
  data in negotiating, 112
  discomfort about, 203–204
  "do this, not that" communication, 139
  expectation of negotiation, 200
  HR and pay discrimination, 36
  Instagram example, 11–12
  leverage and, 209–217
  principles of, 196, 221–224
  productivity and, 26
  profit priority and, 22, 25–26
  strategies for asking, 206–207, 219–221
  what you can negotiate, 224–227
  who is getting the money, 201–204

people, problem with
  communication, 39–49
  reframing, 49–55
  you are part of the problem, 40–41
performance
  about, 12–13
  decoding your manager, 61–62
  development plan, self-directed, 71–76
  feedback, self-directed, 76–81
  how you are perceived, 58–60, 80
  manager behavior clues, 62–65
  manager communication clues, 65–69
  performance reviews and talent rankings, 69–71
performance plan inconsistency angle, 36
perks gap, 100
permission, waiting for, 162
pivots, 290–291
playing the gap. *See* gaps
politics
  about, 14, 267–270
  autonomy principle, 277–279
  innovation principle, 279–281
  line of sight principle, 276–277
  observing, 270–273
  politics report card, 271–272
  risk principle, 281–282
  speed principle, 274–276
power and influence. *See also* gaps
  about, 13
  case studies, 108–109
  Cubicle Guy example, 103–106, 118
  curiosity and, 104–105, 107
  data as, 109–115
  formula for influence, 106–109

information gathering and
knowledge, 115–118
"Stops" and "Starts," 107
working hard vs. playing the gap
and, 83–86
"Power of Starting with 'Yes,' The"
(Schwartz), 174
precedents, 31, 35
predictability of companies, 20–22
prioritization, 161–162, 247–250,
263–264
problem solving
in conflict, 128, 137–138
gaps and, 89–91, 98–99, 102–103
process questions, 159
productivity
burnout and, 261
decision fatigue and, 264
as feeling, 28
myths about, 255–258
pay raise requests and, 26
professional affiliations, 116
profit as company priority, 22,
24–29, 229
promotion and career growth
about, 13, 143–146
data and, 113
halfway conversations and, 48
overachievers and, 150
patterns of people, 146–147
the quickly promoted and, 151
reframing and, 51–53
skill deficiencies by stage, 147–150
Stage 1 (entry level/the doers),
156–161
Stage 2 (supervisors and individual
contributors/the achievers),
161–165
Stage 3 (mid-level professionals/
the collaborators), 170–177

Stage 4 (directors and vice
presidents/the builders),
181–185
Stage 5 (senior vice presidents and
C-suite/the expanders), 185–193
the tentative and, 150–151
proposals, 113, 181

Q
quarterly results, 116
question-asking, 158–159, 223
quick validates, 77–78

R
Ramsey, Dave, 89
recruitment, 48, 90–93, 100,
108–109
reframing
about, 7–8
beliefs quiz, 54–55
meaning of, 50–51
of politics, 282–283
promotions and, 51–53
revising beliefs, 49–50
Regan, Brian, 69–70
reinventing your career, 289
remote work schedules, 224
resources
battle for, 184–185
scarcity of, as leverage, 214
results angle, 32–33
results vs. feelings, 27–28
return on investment (ROI), 27, 111
rework, requests for, 62
risk
HR and, 33–37
as leverage, 214–215
politics of, 281–282
speaking up and, 41–43
in values analysis, 297, 300

Robert Half, 227
Rule of 33, 191–192

S

Schwartz, Tony, 174, 261
security values, 296
senior careers
   about, 9
   disconnected executive fallacy,
      190–193
   gap case study, 93–95
   listening ecosystem, 186, 188–190
   resources, battle for, 184–185
   Rule of 33, 191–192
   skill deficiencies in, 148–149
   Stage 4 (directors and vice
      presidents/the builders),
      181–185
   Stage 5 (senior vice presidents and
      C-suite/the expanders), 185–193
   strategic planning, 182–185, 194
senior vice presidents and C-suite/
   the expanders (Stage 5), 1
   85–193
Habits of Highly Effective People, The
   (Covey), 90, 134
severance
   case study, 176–177
   negotiated, 35, 36, 212, 219, 226
Sharer, Kevin, 188
silos, 171, 173, 175–176
social media recruitment, 92–93,
   108–109
speaking up. *See* communication and
   speaking up
speed, politics of, 274–276
speed gap, 100
steady workers, 84–85
stock options, 226
strategic planning, 182–185, 194

structured programs angle, 36
supervisors and individual
   contributors/the achievers
   (Stage 2), 161–165
Switzler, Al, 134

T

tactical vs. strategic approach,
   182–183, 194
Taft, Michael, 260
talent management, 71–76, 84–85
talent rankings, 70–71
teams, 47, 75, 113, 171–172
10 percent miracle, 239–243
Tesla, 279–280
time management, 240–243
time-off policies, 159
time tracking, 62
time-wasters, 241–242
titles, 103, 105, 225–226
top performers
   doing the right work, 238
   key questions, 159
   leverage and, 215
   loyalty and, 235
   new manager case study, 217–218
   performance reviews and, 70–71
   playing in the gap and, 85
   politics and, 273, 275
   promotability and, 147
   reframing and, 50
   responsibility and, 257
   in talent rankings, 71
training
   in development plans, 74
   the education gap, 100
   negotiating for, 224–225
   questions about, 159
truths
   about burnout, 253

about communication, 39–41
about companies, 19
about conflict, 121, 125
about interdependence, 167
about leaving a job, 285
about leverage, 209
about loyalty, 229
about pay, 195, 203
about performance, 57–59
about politics, 267
about power, 103–106, 118
about promotability, 143, 155
about speed, 179
about working hard, 83–86
freedoms from, 8
of the workforce, 10–14, 304

U
Uber, 279
ultimatums, 222
UnitedHealthcare, 274

V
vacation, preplanned, 225
value added vs. job descriptions,
    83–84, 88–89
value propositions, compelling, 214
values analysis, 295–301
vendor negotiations, 113
Vivint Solar, 191, 277

W
warning indicators, 14–17
WeWork, 281–282
"what we didn't know" gap, 101

Y
"yes," 174–177

ABOUT THE AUTHOR

TESSA WHITE is known as the Job Doctor on social media and has amassed more than one million followers who seek her advice on career navigation strategies. She is a former Fortune 50 executive and a twenty-five-year human resources expert in building people strategies for fast-growth companies with a millennial mindset. She was named in *USA Today* as one of the top entrepreneurs to be inspired by in 2022. Her thought leadership on the modern workplace makes her a frequent guest on national television shows and in top-tier publications.